POWER AND COUNTERPOWER

Labour and Society International
Series Editor: Arthur Lipow, Michael Harrington Centre, Birkbeck College, University of London, and Labour and Society International (LSI).

On the eve of the twenty-first century, a new global economy dominated by transnational corporations is coming into existence. The aim of the Labour and Society International series is to examine the nature of this new global economic order and to explore ways in which the democratic labour movement can offer a response to it: a response based on the politics and ethics of international social solidarity, the defence of human rights, including trade union rights, gender and racial equality, and the right to resist economic and political repression.
The series is a project of Labour and Society International (LSI). Based in London, LSI works with the international trade union movement on these and related issues.

Already published

Socialism: Past and Future
Michael Harrington

Coping with the Miracle: Japan's Unions Explore New Industrial Relations
Hugh Williamson

Breaking Point: A Guide to Preventing Occupational Overuse Syndrome
In association with the International Federation of Chemical, Energy and General Workers' Unions (ICEF)

Economic Fundamentalism
Jane Kelsey

POWER AND COUNTERPOWER

The Union Response to Global Capital

Pluto Press

LONDON • CHICAGO, ILLINOIS

In association with the
**International Federation of Chemical, Energy,
Mine and General Workers' Unions (ICEM)**

First published 1996 by Pluto Press
345 Archway Road, London N6 5AA
and 1436 West Randolph,
Chicago, Illinois 60607, USA

British Library Cataloguing in Publication Data
A catalogue record for this book is available from the British Library

ISBN 0 7453 1113 X pbk

Library of Congress Cataloging in Publication Data
Power and counterpower: the union response to global capital.
     p.   cm. – (International labour series)
     "In association with the International Federation of Chemical,
Energy, Mine and General Workers' Unions (ICEM)."
     1. Trade-unions. 2. Economic history—1990–   3. Capitalism.
4. Competition, International. I. International Federation of
Chemical, Energy, Mine and General Workers' Unions. II. Series.
HD6451.P68   1996
331.88—dc20   95–52766
                                                        CIP

Designed and produced for Pluto Press by
Chase Production Services, Chipping Norton, OX7 5QR
Typeset from disk by Stanford DTP Services, Milton Keynes
Printed in the EC by J.W. Arrowsmith Ltd, Bristol

Contents

About the ICEM

Some 20 million workers worldwide are organised within the International Federation of Chemical, Energy, Mine and General Workers' Unions (ICEM). Headquartered in Brussels, the ICEM is a rapidly growing industry-based trade union federation dedicated to practical international solidarity.

Its main focuses are:

- provision of information on topics ranging from collective bargaining to health and safety standards
- solidarity support for member unions during industrial disputes
- trade union training and union-building programmes.

The ICEM represents workers in energy, mining and quarrying, chemicals, pharmaceuticals, biotechnology, rubber, glass, pulp and paper, cement, ceramics, environmental services and a number of other sectors. Affiliated to it are national industrial trade unions in its sectors on all continents. In January 1996, 403 trade unions in 113 countries were members of the ICEM.

The ICEM has pioneered new techniques of information exchange between affiliated trade unions, including computer networking. In particular, it is expanding trade union contacts and cooperation within the worldwide operations of the major multinational companies in its industries. It issues a range of general and specialised publications. Details on request. The ICEM often makes representations on workers' behalf to national authorities and international bodies. These include the relevant specialised UN agencies, such as the International Labour Organisation and the World Health Organisation. It also takes part in international consultations with corporate managements where appropriate.

International Federation of Chemical, Energy, Mine and General Workers' Unions
avenue Emile de Béco 109, 1050 Brussels, Belgium.
Telephone +32.2.6262020
Fax +32.2.6484316
Internet icem@geo2.poptel.org.uk

Introduction: Global Trade Unionism – a movement on the move

1995 may well have marked a turning point for the world's workers and their trade unions. It was a year of regrouping and rethinking, a year that heralded a trade union come-back – perhaps even a trade union fight-back.

Signs of this new spirit can be seen at the local, national and regional levels. In many countries, industrial union amalgamations promise increased effectiveness, and there is a welcome shift of emphasis back towards organising the unorganised parts of the workforce. National trade union centres are also undergoing change. An important case in point was the election, in October 1995, of a new team to the leadership of the American labour federation AFL-CIO.

Most crucially, trade unions now accept that, in a global economy dominated by transnational corporations (TNCs), labour too must organise globally. Without this worldwide dimension, any trade union revival would be outdated and short-lived. But, as the reports published in this book demonstrate, global organisation is not the same as international organisation.

Trade union internationalism has a history reaching back to the nineteenth century, and its structures are well established. In recent decades, however, those structures have been creaking. If organised labour is really to face up to the one-world economy, if it is to provide at least some social counterweight to the might of the multinationals, then the action of the international trade union movement must be reviewed and renewed. It must become a global trade union movement.

In some cases, those changes are already well under way.

The documents that we have gathered in this small volume are highly significant. Two of them formed the background to a world trade union Congress held in Washington DC on 22 November 1995. The third, adopted unanimously that day by trade union delegates from 96 countries, is the founding declaration of a new industrial trade union international, the

International Federation of Chemical, Energy, Mine and General Workers' Unions (ICEM).

The ICEM is the result of a merger between two union internationals of proven worth – the International Federation of Chemical, Energy and General Workers' Unions (ICEF) and the Miners' International Federation (MIF). Representing some 20 million workers worldwide, the ICEM is a strong new global federation of industrial trade unions in a wide range of sectors. Its coverage is mainly in energy, mining and quarrying, chemicals and bio-science industries, pulp and paper, rubber, glass, ceramics, cement and environmental services. It therefore embraces many of the industries that will play a central role in the future of this planet.

However, the strength of the new international's arguments will be just as important as the argument of its strength. It has been founded on a cogent and original analysis of the modern world. That view is set out very clearly in 'World Social Economy 1995', one of the ICEM background documents that we publish here.

Of course, the finest analysis is of little use unless it is acted upon. So what is to be done? The second ICEM document, 'Unite and Organise', gives some answers. In doing so, it takes a fresh and stimulating look at trade union strategies – and it pledges that the ICEM will be 'the forerunner of the new global institutions of labour'.

One of its central arguments is that industrial trade unionism should concentrate its limited resources on its main tasks – organising workers and improving their pay and conditions. Far from being a limited goal, as some may believe, this consistent pursuit makes the labour movement a force for fundamental political and social change. This connection between medium-term and broader, longer-term goals is recognised in the insistence of 'Unite and Organise' that industrial unions must make strategic use of their strength: 'It should be the trade unions that promote sustainable, democratically decentralised patterns of industrial development – in stark contrast to the exploitative, over-centralised approach of the big corporations'. In that context, its suggestions for international trade union alliances with other social groups are very much to the point.

Equally important is its line on union-building, in other words 'help for self-help by workers who are setting out to organise unions'. Here, the thrust is towards modest but effective assistance for genuinely home-grown trade union movements in the newly-industrialising countries. In the recent past, promising new trade union movements have actually been split by the sudden arrival of outside 'assistance'. Often, this disservice has been done through clumsiness and inexperience. Sometimes, regrettably, it has been deliberate. But whatever the intentions, it is clear that simply throwing money at a new trade union will not help it, and may actually destroy it. Outside expertise can be of genuine assistance, but only when it is offered in the full awareness that it is of limited relevance to the situation of other people in other countries.

The ICEM's warnings against 'trade union imperialism' are therefore timely. Its alternative is regionalisation of some aspects of trade union work. It will have to 'decentralise some activity while maintaining worldwide cohesion and identity'. That is a difficult balance to strike, but one that will be well worth the effort.

Finally, 'Unite and Organise' is important because it foreshadows further change within global trade unionism: 'An ICEF/MIF merger is one step towards greater international trade union unity.'

For readers unfamiliar with the international trade union movement, this requires some explanation. The new ICEM is one of the International Trade Secretariats (ITS). These ITS group, at the international level, national trade unions in the various sectors. Thus, there are separate ITS for metalworkers, for transport workers, for teachers, for public service workers and so on. A full list of the ITS is given in the Appendix.

'Unite and Organise' argues that 'a logical structure would be to group industrial union Internationals within some form of cooperative relationship'. This would indeed be logical – not least in terms of maximising the benefits from limited resources. Indeed, a sympathetic outside observer might wonder if the number of ITS will not be drastically reduced through further amalgamations within the foreseeable future. For example, the process and manufacturing industries are now so closely intertwined, both technically and in terms of ownership, that a rationalisation of national and global union structures in these sectors seems inevitable.

The report also calls for a 'firmer definition' of the 'respective roles of the ITS and the International Confederation of Free Trade Unions (ICFTU)'. The ICFTU is the international grouping of the national trade union confederations. It came into being at the onset of the Cold War, after a split with the communist-led World Federation of Trade Unions (WFTU). After the collapse of communism in Central and Eastern Europe, the WFTU lost most of its funding and its constituency, so that the ICFTU is now undoubtedly the major international confederation of national trade union centres. 'Unite and Organise' argues that the ICFTU should provide 'a progressive, identifiable trade union voice within the intergovernmental agencies' (for instance, the various specialised agencies of the United Nations), while ITS action 'should be focussed mainly on the industry and enterprise level'.

Trade unions are enthusiastic adopters of reports and declarations. Most of these, deservedly or undeservedly, pass into oblivion. We are convinced that the documents in this volume are in a different category. If acted upon, they will prove truly historic.

Arthur Lipow
Editor and Co-Director,
Labour and Society International (LSI)

1. The World Social Economy 1995

In the past two decades, international industrialists and financiers have changed the structure and functioning of the world economy. They have in effect changed the governance of the world and, in doing so, have challenged the institutions, practices and structures which had grown up within the framework of nation states and national economies over the past one hundred years.

This process is often called 'globalisation' but it is, in fact, a 'corporatisation' of political and economic affairs. It is corporatisation because it is the expression of dominance by the multinational corporations, whose production and trading systems and financial operations have been consolidated at the global level. This central position of the multinational corporations in the world economy needs to be understood by trade unionists in order to devise strategies to control the new situation in the interests of their members and to promote social justice and authentic democracy.

The changes associated with this corporatisation issue from precisely those private commercial organisations at the global level which are shielded from the democratic processes of monitoring and social accountability before civic society. These processes of control were in the past most effectively developed in relation to national, rather than international, activities.

This watershed change in the structure of the world economy and civic control has been disguised by announcing the arrival of the so-called 'global economy' or 'the global market' or simply an ill-defined process of 'globalisation'. Yet what has happened may not herald the advent of globalisation in the sense of a more unified, integrated, or cooperative world. So-called 'globalisation' is skewed in its effects and in fact generates conflict, poverty and social injustice over the greater part of the globe. The reason for this is that it is presided over by a relatively small number of multinationally operating corporations which owe no allegiance to state or society.

Multinational corporations are essentially large organisations devoted to bringing about monopoly or oligopoly conditions on a world scale. Through that activity, they have become the most important global organisations in determining investment, finance and trade.

Various UN statistics provide sufficient evidence of this development:

- In 1993 the production in place of the 170,000 subsidiaries of multinational corporations was greater by 37 per cent than the total volume of world trade between nations. World trade in that year totalled $4 trillion, while the total of local sales by the multinational company subsidiaries was a massive $5.5 trillion.
- More than half of that world trade is, in any case, produced by multinational corporations.
- More than one-third of what is counted as world trade is composed of goods transfers within different branches of the same multinationals.
- Two-thirds of all international transactions in goods and services combined are dependent on multinational company operations.

The World Investment report of the UN Conference on Trade and Development (UNCTAD) summarised these developments in the following words: 'This means that most economic transactions no longer take place between independent agents governed by market forces....'[1]

But more important than the official statistics is the power which strategic investment has handed to the multinational companies. Thus the same UNCTAD report notes: ' ... controlling such a pool of assets and stock of investment, the largest TNCs[2] exercise a considerable impact on home and host countries' output, demand patterns, trade and technology flows, employment and labour practices.'

The visible side of this power nexus is the control it gives over technological innovation, over investment patterns and decisions, over the success or failure of national and inter-national environmental efforts, over the effectiveness of health and safety provisions and over the pattern of industrial wages. The largely hidden side is the manipulation of exchange rates, the bribes to government and corporate officials, the destabil-isation of national political structures deemed unfavourable to multinational company objectives, the encouragement of any national repression of and covert resistance towards trade unions, the harassment of critics and the exploitation of unpro-tected workers through increased outsourcing.

Virtual or social? Two realities, two economies

The result of this change in global power relations means that there are now two world economies. There is the 'world virtual economy' of the international financial agencies, the stock market pages, bankers and multinational corporations in which the performance index in any given period is composed of the statistics of economic growth or decline, rises or falls in world trade, numbers of investment locations and the returns on profit and interest.

Then there is the human reality – what we have called the 'world social economy'. This can be measured by how many people are rich and how many poor, how many people are employed and how many out of a job, how many people have had their wages increased and how many have had them cut, how many people's social and health services have been improved and how many have seen them decline, how many people are experiencing a better environment and how many are being poisoned by environmental deterioration, how many people's safety and health are being properly protected at work and how many people are killed, injured or made seriously ill by lax workplace health and safety standards.

The balance sheets for the two economies are different – for the virtual economy it is the short-term growth of output and *average* income; for the social economy it is the *distribution* of wealth and of income, and the *access* to welfare and social justice.

These two economies were never in balance, of course, but in the last two decades they have begun to move in completely opposite directions. More economic growth has brought greater unemployment. Greater worker productivity has brought lower rewards. Greater national incomes have produced poorer health services, less education and fewer social benefits. In short, greater poverty and deeper distress. In the past, nationally based enterprises formed the cornerstone of the world economy. The democratic control of the activities of these enterprises could be achieved both through national laws and regulations and through the effective use of trade union strength. On the new international playing field of production and trade, large corporate organisations effectively escape these national democratic checks and balances. So far there is no world government or institution able or willing to enforce account-ability and social responsibility. Corporatisation thrives on the democratic deficit of the new world order.

The 'virtual reality' of the world production economy for the last few years shows a more positive picture than for many previous years. After five years of zero or negative growth, 1994 and 1995 are supposed to have produced a modest increase in average per person income (see Table 1). Some of this growth has been concentrated in countries which have had generations of slow growth and persistent poverty and the growth of recent years represents the first departure from centuries of stagnation.

Table 1: World Output Grows Again

	1988	1989	1990	1991	1992	1993	1994	1995
Growth in world income per head %	2.8	1.5	0	−1.4	−0.9	−0.6	0.6	1.3

Yet the 'human reality' of the world social economy puts this limited growth into the context of costs and balances. World economic growth in recent years has been positive at the level of manufacturing and services, but growth in food production went down between 1992 and 1993 and is now back to 1980 levels (see Table 2). Economic growth is clearly not diminishing global hunger. Dogmatic marketism has not been able to meet humanity's most basic needs.

Table 2: Index of World Food Production Per Person

1980	1988	1989	1990	1991	1992	1993	1994
100	103	105	106	104	104	102	100

More importantly there has been no progress in re-establishing the returns to national producers of food and commodities which slumped at the end of the 1970s. Still 'the rich get richer and the poor get poorer'. Even the most conservative commentators no longer seek to hide the fact that the current period of world social history is characterised by a worsening distribution of income at both the international and the national levels.

The global rich and poor: further apart than ever

At the global level income distribution was always bad. Now it is getting worse. In 1960 the richest 20 per cent of people in the world had an income 30 times greater than that of the poorest 20 per cent; but by 1991 this ratio had doubled to 60 times. In just 30 years of so-called 'development' the richest 20 per cent had thus increased their share of world income from 70 per cent to 85 per cent while the poorest 20 per cent saw their meagre income shrink from 2.3 per cent to only 1.4 per cent (see Figure 1).

The disparity between different countries and different regions is even more stark. In the broadest, and therefore the crudest, terms it can be said that, taken on aggregate, Africa has

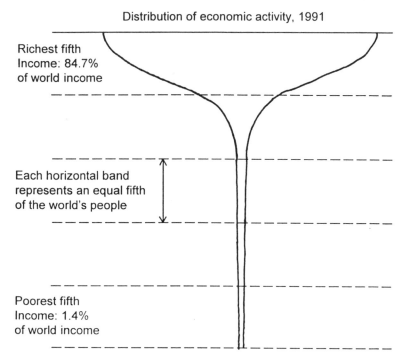

Figure 1. World Income Disparity

continued its decline in the level of income generated and the countries of Central and Eastern Europe have undergone a severe downturn as their industrial economies are reoriented (see Figure 2). Some countries of Asia have, at the same time, produced record-breaking growth statistics (see Table 3). The rich developed market economies have just been able to maintain positive growth.

For the world social economy, the regional disparity produces migratory pressures and graduated systems of global exploitation. It is these disparities which have produced the underlying trade wars and which, above all, create disarray at the regional level, where cooperation and solidarity in the world social economy are badly needed and arguably the easiest to organise.

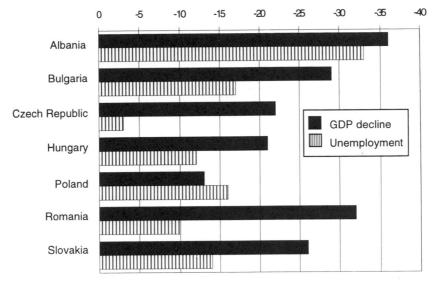

Percentage GDP decline and percentage unemployed

Source: UN/DESIPA and ECE.

Figure 2. Eastern European Economies: Fall in Income and Employment Since 1989

Table 3: Income Growth Selected Asia; Per Cent Annual Change

	1988	1989	1990	1991	1992	1993	1994
South and East Asia	5.9	6.1	6.4	5.3	5.2	5.4	6.0
China	9.9	4.3	3.9	8.0	13.2	13.4	10.0
Developed Economies	2.8	3.3	2.4	0.7	1.6	1.0	2.2

The national rich and poor: turning the clock back

From the point of view of the world social economy, however, the most important regression it has made in the past two decades is the increasing disparity between rich and poor

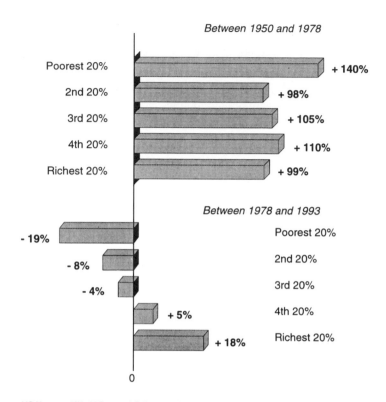

Source: US News and World Report, 6 February 1995

Figure 3. Real Income of Households in the USA, 1950–78 and 1978–93

within individual nations. And in most cases the poorest of the poor are women.

Commentators wedded to the conventional view of the economy merely state that profits have risen faster than wages. This is only part of the story and reveals little about the human reality.

Almost everywhere in the world, income has increased for the top 10 or 20 per cent of the population and decreased for the bottom 20 or even 40 per cent. In the richer economies this has occurred during a period in which the economies themselves have been growing, albeit slowly. In the poorer countries, however, it has occurred during a decade in which the economies were not growing at all. Yet the incomes of the rich still continued to grow in those societies, thus making the losses for the poor even greater.

How has such a situation been brought about? Clearly there have been income increases for the rich and income declines for the poor. Increased profits and dividends help a small percentage of those at the top. But the laxity and the structure of self-payment for high salary earners, which reduced resistance from social organisations, has flooded the world with gift packages to the privileged and already-wealthy. The high-profile cases show astronomical salary increases, but below that are the golden handshakes, golden parachutes, exorbitant professional consulting fees and vast unnecessary increases in the numbers of highly-paid directors.

Recently, a study was made of the impact of the North American Free Trade Agreement (NAFTA) on 26 US firms with more than 1500 employees in Mexico in connection with the NAFTA development. In 1994 the pay package of the Chief Executive Officers of these companies averaged US$2,651,825 each, an average increase of one-third from 1993. Following the collapse of the Mexican peso at the beginning of 1995, workers earning the minimum wage in the Mexican factories of the same US companies saw the dollar value of their pay slump by 40 per cent to the equivalent of US$3.41 per day.

The major reduction in income among the poorer groups has come from the increase in unemployment, decrease in social security payments, declining real income for pensioners, cuts in concessions from privatised services, increased interest rates and wage cuts, whether induced by inflation or as straight-forward 'give-backs'.

These austerity measures affect women and men differently, as women are generally responsible for children, taking care of the elderly and the family's health. Women's labour contribution is considered to be elastic, to meet needs in any eventuality.

Table 4: 'Wage Dispersion' in Selected 'High Income' Countries (ratio of lowest wage in top 10 per cent to upper wage in bottom 10 per cent)

	1980	1986	1991
Australia	2.02	2.21	2.29
France	3.27	3.35	–
Germany	–	2.38	2.31 *(1990)*
UK	2.51	2.97	3.35
USA	4.81	5.55	5.69 *(1989)*
Norway	2.06	2.16	1.97
Japan	–	2.17	2.86 *(1990)*

Source: OECD

More efficiency: less reward

The worldwide trend of redistribution of income towards the rich contains a further irony and injustice – it is occurring at the same time as increased productivity of labour almost everywhere. This means that through greater effort, skill, more demanding methods of work and better machinery, workers everywhere are producing more and more in fewer and fewer hours.

In the social economy it means harder work for less reward – a situation which has been expressed by the following favourite management school equation: 'Productivity = 3/0.5 x 2'. This translates as: 'Half as many people being paid twice as much for working three times as hard.'

In the period 1950–1980 productivity grew annually at rates of between 3 to 6 per cent for a large number of countries. During the same period, workers (on aggregate) received increased wages or improved public services and social security benefits similar to, or above, the value of productivity increases – essentially, a redistribution in favour of wage earners. Since the end of the 1970s, productivity has continued to increase somewhat every year, although at rates lower than in the early period. In certain sectors, limits to productivity increase have started to appear. However, these increases in productivity now accrue disproportionately to the rich. Wage earners have been receiving less than their contribution to productivity increases – in other words, there has been a redistribution away from wage-earners.

To make sure this simple fact is not understood, it is wrapped in impenetrable jargon. Here is how it is expressed in an official economist-written European Union document: 'Since 1980, the real product wage has risen at a slower rate than productivity growth, so causing value-added to shift back (from wages) towards profits.'[3]

Almost everywhere across the world, labour productivity has increased in the past two decades. That it has increased at different rates in different countries is one of the important factors behind the headlines of so-called international competition. Japan's productivity growth (and now that of the recently industrialised countries) has risen at a greater rate than the European and North American increases. These are the basic facts that outline the developments in the 'virtual reality' world of investment, finance and exchange rates.

Interestingly, one way in which this failure to keep wage gains in line with productivity has been engineered by corporations – and by the anti-union governments they dominate – has been to appeal to 'competitivity' between nations in regard to unit labour costs. In motivating their structural adjustment programmes, the bureaucrats of the International Monetary Fund (IMF) argue that the so-called 'relative unit labour cost index' (RUL) must be adjusted to achieve the lowest cost in the world in order to 'be competitive' with other economies. In the richer industrialised economies comparative labour costs are published and republished to indicate the need for a downward wage pressure, accompanied by an upward trend for intensity of work.

Elsewhere in business journals and economic textbooks 'high social labour costs' or 'non-wage costs' are cited negatively. This means that past achievements in the social economy for the humanisation of work and social security provisions to protect people from individual and economic events beyond

Source: Bureau of Labor Statistics

Figure 4. Employee Compensation Costs Index (USA=100). (Production
Workers in Industry)

their control are regarded by some as being 'too expensive', because somewhere else in the world exists a country, a regime or a company which provides even less protection.

The main objective of the discussion around 'competitivity' is to secure downward pressures on wages and benefits by those at the top of the labour costs table without invoking an upward push by those at the bottom.

It is clear that the wage and benefits gap between countries will not be closed for decades, if ever. It is also clear that differences in manufacturing wages between countries will not disappear for a long time. Pay for the same job in one country may be as much as 50 times higher than in another. In the textile industry, for example, workers in Vietnam receive DM 0.42 per hour compared with DM 27 in Germany.

What is not acceptable, even in the short term, is that these facts of development, past exploitation and accident are used to create 'competition' between different national workers with the purpose of producing greater income for multinational companies, their shareholders and their top management, which is not redistributed to society as a whole.

The globalisation of social injustice: the South is everywhere

Structural adjustment, supply-side economics, monetarism, austerity, no-nonsense, flexibility and market-based policies, are just some of the names for the collection of policies which have turned back the clock of our 'human reality' almost 50 years and which demand all our strength to correct. Above all, they have ensured that the rich get richer and the rest get poorer.

These policies have been pursued everywhere across the globe. 'Economic Darwinism' has been spread as an ideology to justify injustice. And injustice is now called 'globalisation'. This is the fashionable word to cover the reality of old-time exploitation. In everyday use it means something different to different groups and more often than not it means nothing at all. Exploitation in any case tends to produce knock-on effects throughout the social economy. For example, given their multiple roles as mothers and breadwinners, the economic exploitation of women affects their families and communities as well as the women themselves.

For multinational corporations, however, globalisation means increased power to shift resources between nation states so as to take advantage of different tax and labour regimes and to move goods around the world without regulation or control. For rich people throughout the world, globalisation means the ability to hold foreign bank accounts without fear of the local taxman, to export capital, to own property, in short, to enjoy the pool of resources which are made available globally for those with money to enjoy them.

For 'free market' ideologues who see always the private interest rather than the public, who see profit rather than welfare, coercion rather than security and consumption rather than con-servation, globalisation means the establishment of 'global markets' in which national, cultural and social resistance to purchasing patterns will be crushed under the integrated weight of world production.

For those who view the world economy in material, rather than in social terms, globalisation has a meaning only in the statistics of the virtual world of economics. Perhaps the most dominant element of that world is the international financial market, in which the transfer of numbers by the touch of a computer keyboard has promoted belief in the existence of a global market. Yet in trade the picture is less clear – world trade has not grown phenomenally and it is still biased in favour of the richer industrial economies. Global labour mobility certainly does not exist – indeed the last few years have seen a signifi-cant closing down of migration channels.

For those who are marginalised in this process, however, or for those who are candidates for marginalisation, globalisation diminishes their power, reduces their wages and destabilises their security and their general quality of life.

It is the ideology of neo-liberalism which has been globalised and in the service of which all power has been skewed towards private interests. Its universal symptoms are privatisation, deregulation, labour market 'flexibility', and reduction of government spending. The insane promotion of competition at all costs is however one of the most pernicious values carried by the ideology of neo-liberalism. Competition carries in itself the negation of solidarity, accountability, collective responsibility for the weak, promotion of equality, consensus building and dialogue which are cornerstones of democratic governance.

Governments in the service of the corporatised economy

The effect of this overwhelming increase in corporate power, in pursuit of global interests, has been to fundamentally undermine significant segments of state administration and to reduce their power both nationally and internationally. Governments are expected to confine their role to the creation of an enabling environment for the unbridled aspirations of corporate power.

Public control has been drained from crucial social institutions. The income distribution status quo has been taken as the base from which all calculations proceed. This has meant that higher taxation on those earning higher incomes to pay for social needs and socially just national projects has been rejected on the grounds that this would destroy 'international competitivity'. Organised exchange-rate raids and speculations against national currencies by corporate financial institutions and multinational company cash managers undermine national budget experiments and fiscal policies.

Abandonment of state-introduced regulations – so-called 'deregulation' – means self-regulation or specific re-regulations on their own terms by corporations of those areas which are of interest to them. Structural adjustment programmes and policy proposals of inter-governmental organisations such as the OECD, World Bank and IMF have been for 'deregulation' and 'flexibility of labour markets' in order to weaken the resistance of workers and their organisations. Yet the same member governments of these institutions, serving multinational corporation interests, have actually *re-regulated* areas such as intellectual property in order to improve the power of the companies themselves to control where and how technology may be used and to whom it may be denied worldwide.

In democratic countries the points of resistance to this process of globalisation through corporatisation have come from the social organisations – in particular, from the trade unions. The well-documented onslaught by right-wing governments which have introduced new, malicious laws and regulations against trade unions is part of the project to eliminate opposition to corporate power – globally.

Table 5: Global Privatisation Revenues 1988–93 (US$ millions)

Region	1988	1989	1990	1991	1992	1993	Total
East Asia and the Pacific	21	2296	376	790	5204	7467	16153
Europe and Central Asia	27	954	2428	3723	6198	4621	17951
Latin America and the Caribbean	2530	1436	7297	17989	15797	10140	55188
Middle East and North Africa	7	14	2	17	70	633	742
South Asia	0	3	29	996	1557	974	3560
Sub-Saharan Africa	10	1450	71	50	178	614	2372
Total: Developing countries	2595	6153	10203	23565	29004	24449	95966
Industrial countries	37550	21486	16880	30399	18728	49896	174938
Total	**40144**	**27639**	**27083**	**53964**	**47732**	**74345**	**270905**

Source: World Bank

No project of the last decades could be more illustrative of this project to corporatise the world economy through weakening state activities than the global 'privatisation' campaign. In the five years between 1988 and 1993, $270 billion of holdings were transferred from state to private hands through this policy of selling state-owned companies to private individuals and companies (see Table 5). Multinational corporations now take the opportunity to purchase strategic enterprises or whole industries at the rate of over $60 billion per year. By 1993, 44 per cent of all revenue from purchases in developing countries was supplied by foreign investors.

Privatisation affects women and men differently. Women suffer twice from privatisation. Public services have traditionally been a source of employment for women. When jobs are cut through privatisation, women are the first to go. Likewise cuts in public services such as childcare, schools and health services affect women more severely because they are generally in charge of their family's welfare.

The sick social economy

The discontinuity between the two economies – the world virtual economy and the world social economy – has produced a sickness. It is producing poverty, unemployment, disease and disaster. The sickness arises because the premises on which the nation state was based no longer hold true. In the conventional view it was accepted that one country did not interfere in the political affairs of another and, if it did so, this would be seen as an act of war or subversion. Yet it is seen neither as an act of war nor as subversion if multinationals stage a capital strike, if banks make a run on the national currency, if overseas investors withdraw their funds overnight, or if companies campaign to weaken popular support for a government that proves sympathetic to the needs of its citizens rather than those of multinational corporation managers.

The sickness is that governments are no longer expected to focus their policies on what is best for the population. Rather, they are expected to prepare the nation to be a suitable and tame site for multinational investors. Governments are, one after another, dropping full employment policies and reducing budgetary means used to combat poverty and exclusion. Macro-economic monetarist policy and budgetary control are the preferred tools in dismantling social protection and welfare.

The production economy continues to offer (except only in the poorest countries of Africa) promises of economic growth and greater income for the already-wealthy. It will continue to do so and to subordinate the human economy for as long as the workers and the general population accept that this should be the case.

Official documents and business analysts now muse on how long this situation can last. The Chase Manhattan Bank newsletter on 'Emerging Markets' hints darkly to investors in relation to the Mexican financial crisis at the end of 1994: 'It also raises the issue of whether or not the Mexican working class will accept a prolonged period of wage losses and diminished living standards.'[4]

A UN Report on the world economy states, concerning unemployment: 'At the social level, unemployment may also exacerbate the polarisation of society into "have" and "have not" groups. ... Chronic unemployment may contribute to the incidence of mass violence and even open warfare.' The use of the word 'may' would seem outrageous to the families and friends of the 593 trade unionists killed for trade union activities in 1994, the 1,935 who were injured and the 66,000 dismissed for daring to belong to a union.

The healing process for the world social economy must start with a programmed rehabilitation. Rehabilitation starts with reassessment. Reassessment starts with comprehending the global aspects of national life.

Multinational investments – consolidation of power

The statistics on foreign direct investment are one of the most quoted and available measures of multinational corporation activity. Like trade statistics, however, foreign direct investment statistics disguise almost as much as they reveal, because they are based on nationally collected data rather than on company level data.

However, if the foreign direct investment statistics demonstrate clear and sizeable trends, they at least provide some idea of activity levels in the purchase and creation of production and service facilities around the world by externally-headquartered companies. In 1993–95, the statistics do indeed reveal some significant trends:

- *The continuing major trend was that the bulk of foreign direct investment was contained within the triad of Japan, North America and the European Union.* The industrialised countries continued to distribute 70 per cent of their total investment among themselves – within the rich industrialised world.

- *Only 10 countries from the South accounted for more than 70 per cent of all the remaining investment* (see Table 6). The most favoured recent investment locations of the South are China, Singapore, Malaysia, Thailand and Brazil – although in comparison with the size of the countries, the per capita development/investment league table is headed by Thailand, followed by Malaysia, Hong Kong and Singapore. Essentially this means that most countries of the South (containing the bulk of humanity) are still not of great interest to multinationals as investment prospects.

- *The big five economies – USA, UK, France, Germany, Japan – continued to dominate over 63 per cent of total world investment and to own 75 corporations out of the top 100* (see Figure 5). What has been referred to as the 'triadisation' of the world continues unabated.

- *The profit picture from world investments has still not changed substantially over the past 10 years.* Despite high profits available in Africa and Asia, the risks of investment in many countries of those regions and the limitations of their markets encourage investment in the 'safer' climates of the richer countries, even though profits there are lower.

Table 6: Ten Largest Host Developing Countries for Foreign Direct Investment 1981–92

Host economy	1981	1985	1986	1988	1989	1990	1991	1992	1981–92
China	–	1659	1875	3194	3393	3487	4366	11156	33768
Singapore	1660	1047	1710	3655	2773	5263	4395	5635	33012
Mexico	2835	491	1523	2594	3037	2632	4762	5366	28992
Malaysia	1265	695	489	–	1668	2332	3998	4469	18794
Brazil	2520	1348	–	2969	1267	901	–	1454	17752
Hong Kong	1088	–	996	2627	1076	1728	–	1918	14665
Argentina	837	919	574	1147	–	1836	2439	4179	12199
Thailand	–	–	–	1105	1775	2444	2014	2116	10205
Egypt	753	1178	1217	1190	1250	–	–	–	7755
Taiwan	–	340	326	959	1604	1330	1271	–	6545
Percentage share of the ten largest host countries in total inflows to developing countries	81	68	70	73	72	74	71	76	72

Source: UNCTAD

What has changed since 1992? Six trends can be noticed:

- *Many multinational corporations have caught 'China fever'.* International traders caught this disease in the 1980s – now it is the turn of international investors. China fever in the past was triggered simply by the prospect of selling into the most massive market in the world. As one businessman stated in 1980: 'I sell pens – I only have to sell one pen to each Chinese to become a mega-size company'. Now the driving force of China fever is a combination of this huge market attraction with the added advantage of producing with a controlled and cheaper labour force.

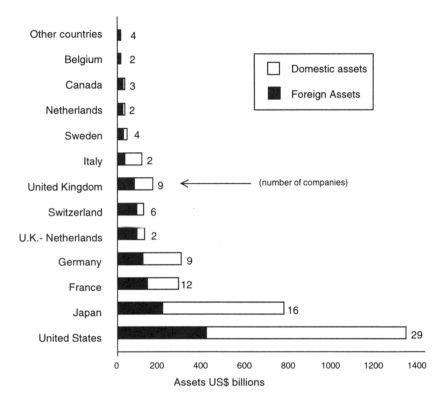

Source: UNCTAD

Figure 5. Top 100 Multinationals: Companies, Assets and Home Country 1992

- Despite the cheap labour attraction of China, it is now clear that *multinational corporation relocation decisions are not focussed principally on cheaper labour.* It is rather the combination of this added benefit with the other major bonuses of market access, resource availability and organisational or political climate which provides a strong interacting set of incentives.

   The greatest repository of cheap labour is in the southern countries, yet it is obvious from the statistics that these countries are *not* the favourite sites for foreign direct investment. The reason is that modern production techniques mostly need highly *skilled* labour which is not so readily available in low wage countries. Transport costs and investment risks have also increased throughout the developing world. In addition the degrading physical, infrastructural and health environments are disincentives for transnational managers facing personal relocation.

■ *After a number of years during which American companies invested less on a world scale than did companies originating in Japan or the UK, the tide has now turned once more.* From 1991 onwards US companies have restored their dominant position in the outflow of direct investment. Estimates for 1993 show that American companies – with $50 billion of outflow – are investing twice as much as any of the other big five investing countries.

Table 7: Profitability* of US Multinational Corporations by Region 1977–91 (percentage)

Region/country	1977	1982	1987	1988	1989	1990	1991
Developed countries	12.5	10.0	16.8	19.9	18.1	15.6	12.8
Canada	9.9	7.2	11.9	13.0	12.1	8.1	4.8
Europe	13.8	11.0	18.9	22.9	20.0	17.6	14.9
Other developed countries	13.7	11.6	14.6	17.0	18.1	15.4	12.2
Developing countries	23.9	14.6	12.9	14.0	17.1	15.9	13.7
Africa	33.2	10.8	14.7	22.9	20.1	22.2	22.7
South, East and Southeast Asia and the Pacific	29.9	34.2	22.3	25.4	26.8	30.1	26.0
Western Asia	–54.2	28.7	8.7	11.1	9.4	19.0	16.4
Latin America and the Caribbean	11.7	10.1	10.7	10.9	14.6	11.4	9.4
All countries	14.6	11.6	15.3	18.0	17.7	15.7	13.0

* Measured by net income as share of owners' equity

Source: UNCTAD

- *The trends for different sectors are volatile.* Mining and petroleum make up 39 per cent of total foreign assets and there seems to be no indication of change. Individual companies in the industry vary considerably, however, as to their policies on investment and disinvestment.

- *Integrated international production is being consolidated and global transaction structures are being developed.* Integrated international production is indicated by intra-company transfers of goods in which semi-finished goods or components are shifted from one subsidiary to another in an international production chain.

  Integrated production has meant that by 1989 over one third of all exports from Japan and the USA were exports from multinationals to subsidiaries and 34 per cent of imports for USA and 30 per cent for Japan were likewise intra-company transfers. In the case of Sweden, the share of intermediate goods to multinational affiliates as a percentage of total intermediate goods shipments rose from 21 per cent in 1974 to 79 per cent in 1990. The main effect of this has been to weaken further any national or international control on global output.

  Global transaction structures are inter-industry transactions which, collectively, make an integrated and dependent megasector. One product industry is dependent upon another product industry. The most obvious example is the relationship between the oil, plastics, rubber and motor industries (see Table 8).

- *There is a noticeable trend towards instability and volatility in the systems of finance and investment.* The flexibility brought by deregulation of capital markets and the reduction in investment rules means that investments are being switched with ever-greater frequency and rapidity. Cycles of investment interest are becoming shorter. The recent flood of investment into China, for example, occurred in the space of just a few years as did the fashionable phase for investment into the USA which preceded it.

This situation is compounded by the clear lack of foresight and the tendency for 'experts' to believe their own propaganda. The markets are blind as bats and typically lack the capacity to take long-term views at the expense of immediate profits. This dominance of 'short-termism' is clearly at the expense of any form of social policy-making.

To take the Mexican example. In November 1994 the OECD was fulsome in its praise for Mexico's attitude towards multi-national corporations: 'The major effort of the Salinas government to liberalise foreign investment can serve as a model for developing countries,' it wrote, and 'The OECD welcomes the commitments entered into by Mexico, and encourages it to continue along the same path'.[5]

Yet less than two months after these words were written the path which was a 'model for developing countries' had led to a collapse of the currency, losses of 30 per cent for foreign investors and a panic bail-out of record-breaking proportions – $40 billion which was secured only through the power of the USA, backed by guarantees that effectively mortgage the whole of Mexico's considerable energy industries.

The Mexican story is illustrative of the lack of accuracy of current business and financial writers who are not concerned or informed about the real human economy. When real people respond to the devastation wrought by the virtual economy on the social economy, the reaction of investors has even been to call in the military. Unfortunately for the virtual realists, the courage of real people in the face of repression is not so easily swept aside.

These trends enable a basic picture of the current and longer-term future of the world economy to be built. 'Globalisation' – as we have sought to demonstrate – is more accurately a process of yielding increased power to the multi-national corporations which are developing integrated production

Table 8: A Global Transaction Structure: The Oil and Auto Industries 1990 (turnover in millions of ECU)

Oil companies			Car and components manufacturers		
Royal Dutch Shell	EC	83034	General Motors	USA	96640
Exxon	USA	82720	Ford Motor	USA	76551
Mobil	USA	46299	Toyota Motor	JPN	53778
British Petroleum	EC	46172	Daimler-Benz	EC	41570
ENI	EC	32882	Fiat	EC	37758
Texaco	USA	32062	Volkswagen	EC	33091
Chevron	USA	30265	Nissan Motor	JPN	32330
Elf Aquitaine	EC	25325	Renault	EC	23664
Amoco	USA	21958	Chrysler	USA	23359
Total	EC	18537	Honda Motor	JPN	23314
Petróleos de Venezuela	VEN	18117	Peugeot	EC	23088
Pemex	MEX	15228	Robert Bosch	EC	15507
Atlantic Richfield	USA	14117	Mitsubishi Motors	JPN	15164
Nippon Oil	JPN	13497	Mazda Motor	JPN	14712
Petrobras	BRA	12219	BMW	EC	13214
Idemitsu	JPN	11272	Volvo	EFTA	11034
Repsol	EC	10922	Isuzu Motors	JPN	8390
Phillips Petroleum	USA	19664	Nippondenso	JPN	8208
USX-Marathon Group	USA	10413	Suzuki Motor	JPN	6780
Petrofina	EC	10229	TRW	USA	6404
Neste	EFTA	9589	Audi	EC	5895
SUN	USA	9260			
Statoil	EFTA	9104			
Showa Shell Sekiyu KK	JPN	8970			
Unocal	USA	8345			
Imperial Oil	CAN	7538			
Ashland Oil	USA	7041			
Nippon Mining Co	JPN	6534			
RWE-DEA	EC	6049			
Mitsubishi Oil	JPN	6029			
Total		633391	Total		570 451

Source: Panorama of EC Industries 1993.

and transaction structures. Multinationals are conservative in their patterns of investment, preferring to place the bulk of their investments in the stable, structured, industrialised economies rather than moving South. When they do shift outside the rich enclaves, however, they seek favoured sites where the driving force is a combination of new markets, resources and a free hand, rather than primarily cheap, unskilled labour. This is one reason why the USA is set to restore its dominant position in terms of investment outflows. Nevertheless, as we have pointed out in earlier sections, and as recent trade union experience clearly shows, the threat of labour 'competitivity' is constantly employed by corporate apologists to maintain downward pressure on pay and conditions in industrialised countries and to counteract labour solidarity.

Multinational corporations are integrating as they become more powerful. As in all such organisations, the dynamic is more towards secrecy than transparency. Multinationals are increasingly resistant to intervention in their internal affairs by law, the state or the unions. Many companies resist trade union organisation, but the motives are not simply the traditional ones connected with control of production processes and labour costs. They are rather part of a general resistance to, and exclusion of, all organisations which may gain a knowledge of the internal practices of the company and seek to exercise an alternative influence over policies.

International trade: the state as agent of the multinational corporation

In the past four years, international trade has been constantly in the news. The Uruguay Round and the birth of the World Trade Organisation have also propagandised the virtues of 'free trade' and extolled the expected benefits.

Essentially there have been no dramatic changes in either the pattern or the size of world trade, except for the massive decline in exports from Eastern European countries (see Table 9). The apparently major event in the world trade arena has been the creation of the World Trade Organisation and the development of regional trading arrangements, such as the European Union (EU), North American Free Trade Agreement (NAFTA), the Latin American Southern Cone Common Market

(MERCOSUR) and the continued discussions surrounding the Asian Free Trade Arrangement (AFTA) and Asia Pacific Economic Community (APEC).

Table 9: World Trade 1984–94: Annual; Percentage Change in Exports

	1984	1985	1986	1987	1988	1989	1990	1991	1992	1993	1994
World	8.3	3.0	5.9	4.7	7.3	8.0	5.6	4.6	5.5	2.7	6.0
Developed market economies	9.6	4.7	2.5	4.4	8.5	7.3	5.1	3.7	4.2	1.3	5.0
Developing countries	5.9	–0.1	15.2	6.6	4.4	11.8	8.7	8.7	8.5	8.3	7.4
Economies in transition	4.9	–0.6	4.3	2.6	4.5	–1.5	–9.5	–18.8	–11.3	–	–
Eastern Europe	7.3	2.0	–0.6	1.7	4.3	–2.9	–6.2	–9.3	–0.1	–5.0	–
Former USSR	2.5	–4.3	10.0	3.4	4.9	0.1	–13.0	–31.0	–22.7	–	–

Source: IMF

Many of the real issues of international trade are hidden because the associated calculations are made on the basis of global models of extraordinary abstraction. The models themselves are constructed on the basis of hundreds of specific assumptions and arrive at the self-fulfilling conclusion that the outcomes negotiated by those who commission the models are to the global benefit. The production economy is satisfied – the human economy is not part of the concern.

These models cannot incorporate the extra-state factors. There is no recognition of the fact that two-thirds of world trade in goods and services are dependent on multinational companies, or that one-third of world trade is in fact straight transfers between subsidiaries of multinationals. If these considerations were included in the calculations, it is clear that the vast majority of goods produced have no relationship whatsoever to concepts of 'free trade'. As these transfers are made at prices determined by the company and created only for the purposes of transferring costs or profits between facilities in a strictly managed pattern, they are not subject to academic fantasy theories which depend on an expert, omniscient buyer operating in a free and competitive market. 'Free trade' for multinationals simply means free to fix international prices and free from government regulation – not free to compete.

The world trade organisation: a lever for the production economy

The General Agreement on Tariffs and Trade (GATT), created in 1947, was based upon the premise that the nation state is the major player in determining the pattern of world trade. Within that view of economics, if a company violates international rules only the state in which it operates can be punished. Under these circumstances any 'punishment' of a multinational company must depend entirely on the willingness of the government to act against the headquarters of a multinational on its territory. Otherwise the punishment will simply be passed on to the consumer, that is, to the people of the nation concerned. In 1995 the successor to GATT, the World Trade Organisation (WTO), was established and, despite the massive changes in the world economy since 1947, the same rules of behaviour were continued – but with some important new aspects added.

There has been a partly hidden agenda for the creation of the WTO. It is the use of the so-called 'trade weapon' to enforce globally the demands and the interests of multinational corporations and their acquiescent governments. The most striking aspect in an investigation of this trade weapon is the wide variation between the size of different economies. Imports into one economy can be as much as 40 times greater than the total output of another (see Table 10). Clearly, therefore, if the companies headquartered within the larger economies can persuade or force their governments to use trade as a weapon, they can apply a powerful tool of enforcement to advance their interests in the economic territories of others.

Table 10: Economic Size, Trade Power and Trade Dependency

	Economy Size, Production(GDP) Billions US $	Trade Power, Imports Billions US $	Trade Dependency (Imports as per cent GDP)
USA	5686.00	553.00	10%
Japan	3337.00	223.00	11%
Italy	1072.00	187.00	20%
Barbados	1.70	.70	49%
Taiwan	180.00	72.00	48%

The new provisions of the WTO are designed precisely to facilitate the use of this weapon to protect the interests of the multinational corporations in investment, patents and services.

Trade and investment: marginalising the national interest

The trade weapon can now be used against countries which, for social, political or other domestic reasons, seek to control, monitor or direct foreign investment. Even some of the more liberalised economies still have restrictions on foreign investment. These restrict activity in areas such as natural resources, transport and audio-visual production, for example. In such cases foreign shareholdings and direct investment must seek government approval. Under the new TRIM agreement (Trade Related Investment Measures), action can eventually be taken in the trade field if any country has regulations relating to investment which are adjudged to hinder trade. Given that, as we have shown, trade also includes substantial intra-company transfers almost any regulation can fall in this category. Thus the TRIMs threaten even the weak remaining investment regulations that some countries have tried to practice.

Complete freedom of investment, eliminating national and governmental control is the basic objective of this measure. As multinationals are the vehicles for 90 per cent of world investment, TRIMs operate as a government-constructed measure to assist the escape of multinational corporations from responsibility and accountability for the nature, operation and direction of their investments. This is a further weakening of national democratic control over national economic life and destiny.

Patents: consolidating technological power

Even more important for the future of the social economy is the WTO's role in controlling the world availability of technology. The power of the major players in the technology field arises from the so-called Trade Related Intellectual Property (TRIPs) measures within the WTO accords. Intellectual property is the name given to the knowledge incorporated in processes and products which emerge on the market as patents and trade marks.

As multinational corporations have grown larger and amassed huge capital reserves, they have been able to devote increasing sums to the Research and Development (R&D) of new products and processes. For large-scale investment in R&D, large-scale organisations are needed and in the past two decades multinationals have replaced publicly-supported universities and research institutes as the funders of R&D. To recoup their R&D expenditures, multinationals must incorporate that expenditure in end-prices or sell patents and derive royalties from licensing the use of trade marks. Currently most new inventions and processes are diffused via controlled subsidiaries: in 1992 over 80 per cent of all receipts for patents, inventions and processes for Germany, the United Kingdom and the USA were from affiliates to parent companies. These were worth at least $30 billion.

However, the problem for multinationals was that significant numbers of patents and inventions were 'escaping' from their control through pirating, imitation and under-reporting. These are precisely the techniques that Japan and later industrialising countries have used in the past to speed their development. Enforcement of patents and licences at the international level was weak and the TRIP arrangements are designed to put teeth into enforcement techniques and enable the developers of technology to control its use and diffusion and, above all, to ensure good returns from it.

Services: a new area of control of the world economy

The other major development of the WTO has been to include services within the framework of the agreement. Services have been the major growth area of international investment and trade in the last five years, to the point where they now comprise 30 per cent of total world trade.

Services include banking, insurance, transport, law and telecommunications. They have never before been subject to any ruling that foreigners must be given equal treatment to nationals. The reason has been that these services, unlike goods, were especially deeply related to national structure, culture, practices and objectives. Now the process has begun to dismantle these national characteristics in favour of those who have the power to supply such services on an international basis.

The WTO provisions make it possible for certain sectors to be singled out and made part of special agreements between nations. Governments can, therefore, commit countries to a future in which banking, insurance or the all-important audio-visual sector may be controlled by specific corporate interests multi-nationally – another example of the use of the trade instrument to secure further corporatisation of the world production economy.

Regional arrangements: geopolitics in disguise

At the same time as the World Trade Organisation has been created, the scramble has begun to create regional trading and political organisations – the so-called regional 'free trade areas', the European Union, the NAFTA/MERCOSUR/AFTA group and APEC. Recent discussions about an eventual Trans-Atlantic Free Trade Area (TAFTA) and links between NAFTA and APEC show rather clearly the real power behind these groupings. The initially slow progress is now gathering speed towards the construction of a 'Free Trade Zone' that rings the globe – within which multinational capital will have a completely free hand.

In all cases the regional arrangements have consolidated neo-liberal policies which argue that nations must compete on the basis of maximum freedom for corporate capital – with dereg-ulated product markets, laxer environmental laws and flexible labour markets. In essence, politicians have been persuaded or co-opted into dismantling the control apparatus of the nation state, in a bid to recreate some semblance of control at the inter-mediate regional level. However, the very fact that these negotiations have had to be concluded by governments rather than by companies has meant that trade unions and other social organisations have been able to gain a certain presence in this process of institutional change. As a result, they have also been able to press for changes in the new arrangements through specific 'side agreements', 'social chapters' or 'social clauses'. Though no longer at the centre of political debate and consideration, social institutions have rather retained a role of important lobbyists within these newly forming structures.

It is already evident, however, that the shift of control, once started, will not be halted at the regional level. While described as 'regionalism', these arrangements are based upon trade con-venience which seldom corresponds to an authentic regionalism based upon geographic, cultural, historical or linguistic simi-larities. As the EU awkwardly embraces countries as diverse as Finland and Greece, it also has one eye on Central and Eastern Europe and the other on North Africa because of the natural attractions of markets, resources, trade and geopolitical strategy (in roughly that order).

At the same time, the 'Free Trade Area of the Americas' strains towards fulfilling the old dream of US dominion over the poor South. Social organisations such as trade unions are stretched to respond from their essentially local and national organising bases with regional structures that mirror the virtual reality of economic regionalism, while it continues constantly to shift and expand to the world level.

The social economy, the social clause and trade

The burden of adjustments needed to accommodate the shifts in international trade has always fallen disproportionately on the weakest groups in the production economy – workers. The production economy claims this sacrifice for the benefit of the whole and for the transfer of benefits – employment in sunrise industries, unemployment in sunset industries.

Trade unions have always resisted the treatment of labour as a flexible factor of production. Via the nation state, unions have sought to include safeguards against such unequal distribution of benefits from trading. These national efforts led to the formation of the International Labour Organisation (ILO) in 1919, in recognition that trade caused social injustice and social injustice caused wars. Now that the nation state has been weakened by international production and transaction structures, the possibility of monitoring the social effects of trade has been raised for possible incorporation into the new structures of the WTO and the regional 'free trade areas'.

Minimally, a 'social clause' would seek to prevent trade in goods produced by workers in countries which refuse to subscribe to the ILO conventions relating to the right to organise and to bargain collectively, and others on forced labour, equality of treatment and child labour. Despite almost universal claims by governments that they already oppose anti-union and inhuman treatment on their territories, there has been considerable opposition at government level to the introduction of 'social clauses' within the central texts of the regional 'free trade' accords. Some suspect a thinly-veiled protectionism – perhaps understandably in view of the real terms of international trade which, as we have argued, overwhelmingly favour the richer nations. Others, however, simply reflect the interests of home-grown entrepreneurs in labour-intensive industries, who intend to maintain the flow of such income as is available from exploited workers to the rich elite.

Effective trade unions formed under the 'freedom to organise' provisions of social clauses might help introduce universal minimum standards for employees in matters of treatment and conditions. A reduction in health and safety protection costs and in social and hourly wages is still a part of the incentive package which encourages companies in certain industries to relocate production. Most multinational corporations, however, as we have seen from the earlier statistics on foreign direct investment, have passed the stage where foreign investment was exclusively, or even substantially, directed towards obtaining cheaper labour. For this reason, acceptance of the social clause has not proved so difficult for the multinational companies as it has for governments. After all, the basic obligation is on the government to enforce such standards – not on the employer. It is also the government that has the problem of providing labour market incentives to world-sourcing multinationals. Agreement would undoubtedly be less forthcoming if the obligation to respect minimum labour standards were placed directly upon multinationals and their subcontractors and some real mechanism developed for their enforcement.

Trade, the social economy and environmental responsibility

While the social clause was not fully accepted in the creation of the WTO, the addition of an environmental condition has been more easily received. The impact of the production economy has been at its most damaging on mankind's natural habitat – the planet. It has resulted in extensive damage to essential planetary natural resources through the multiplication of greenhouse gases in the atmosphere, accumulation of acids in soil and water, radioactivity, permanent and polluting chemicals and the ongoing destruction of bio-diversity. Workers themselves have immensely and directly suffered from this onslaught on the world's resources. In developing countries, women are particularly affected by environmental degradation, as they have to fetch water and firewood.

Unless urgent action is agreed upon, workers' children will also be the first to suffer from this damage. It would, however, be a sad and unacceptable irony if, as a result of environmental protection measures, workers suffered further from hastily designed regulations and plant closures. Environment protection and the promotion of energy conservation and efficiency should become employment-creating sectors.

The only response to this environmental pillage at the international level has been from general guidelines and agreements at the level of principle, but with weak enforcing mechanisms. The creation of a trade and environment committee to monitor and deploy WTO provisions for environmental considerations is at least a recognition that international efforts at environmental protection are necessary.

Finance and debt: maintaining the transfers

The world virtual economy continues to transfer resources from the poorer citizens of the world to the richer. The basic 'returns' from global economic transactions are profits on investment and trade, royalties and interest on debt. These are the counterparts of the 'outflows' of direct investment, indirect investment (through stocks and shares), loans and technology licensing agreements.

A final balance of outflow and returns, referenced earlier, shows that the global rich receive income from the global poor.

Resource flows: underwriting the high spenders

The pattern of resource transfers between countries is key to understanding current world politics. The very basic pattern over recent years has been that the UK and USA are drawing in financial resources from Japan, Germany and the developing countries. Japan in particular has been consistently supporting inflows to the USA over the past ten years (see Table 11).

The flows of financial support from Japan and Germany to the two other major investors, the USA and the UK, are the background to continuing trade and interest rate disputes between the big four.

Table 11: Resource Transfers from Japan 1984–93

	1984	1986	1988	1989	1991	1992	1993[a]
OECD countries of which:	−40.8	−67.1	−54.8	−37.7	−39.5	−52.7	−48.1
USA	−33.7	−50.6	−40.6	−33.3	−23.0	−30.2	−39.5
European Union of which:	−8.0	−14.5	−18.0	−10.4	−24.3	−29.3	−19.0
United Kingdom	−1.4	−2.2	−3.7	−0.8	−6.3	−9.6	−4.5
Germany[b]	–	–	−7.6	−6.5	−9.1	−8.9	−7.1
Transition economies[c]	−3.3	−6.5	−0.8	−0.0	1.2	1.2	1.2
Developing countries	11.9	−4.8	−7.0	−0.2	−20.4	−34.4	−50.3

Source: UN/DESIPA, based on Bank of Japan, Balance of Payments Monthly.

a. Secretariat estimate based mainly on customs trade data.
b. Including transactions with the eastern Länder of Germany from October 1990.
c. Including China until 1987.

The major change in financial flows over the past five years is that the developing countries moved from a net outflow in 1990 of $30 billion to an inflow in 1992 of $42 billion. This fact has been hailed by the uninformed as 'the end of the debt crisis'. This is sadly very far from being the case – all it means is that the flow of new loans and direct investment was greater during these years than repayments of debt and interest on old loans and the repatriation of profits. In short, financial flows which appear positive are in fact taking place under conditions which are simply deepening developing country indebtedness in the longer term and which constitute continued high basic transfers from the poor economies to the rich (see Table 12).

Despite the recent spurt of investment and activity in southern countries by the multinational corporations, the rich country banks and governments still receive more in interest than do the multinationals in profit – a reversal of the situation since 1970. This is a fundamental fact of the virtual economy and implies that the social economy must continue to pay a high price for past (unproductive) loans. When the basic calculations of returns are made, it is still the case that profit and interest drawn into the richer countries are three times as much as the so-called 'aid' given to the poorer countries (see Table 13).

Table 12: Profit and Interest from the Third World

| | Billion US Dollars | | | | | | | |
	1970	1980	1987	1990	1991	1992	1993	1994
Interest	2.4	35.1	57.6	59.4	60.3	57.4	57.6	64.5
Profit	6.5	24.0	12.5	17.8	18.5	21.3	23.3	25.4

Source: World Bank

Table 13: Transfers from Poor Countries to Richer Countries 1992

Interest on debt due	$125 billion
Estimate of return (profit) on investment of multinationals 15% of $420b (stock of investment)	$64 billion
Total	$189 billion
Minus 'aid' granted	$59 billion
Worth of poor countries to rich	**$130 billion**

Source: ICEM calculation from UNCTAD: World Investment Report 1994, World Bank Debt Tables 1994

Third world debt: part of globalisation

The debt crisis was really only a crisis for the lending countries, who were scared that they would not get their interest and loans repaid: now that fear is more-or-less over. The Latin American and Asian economies have been restructured into effective debt servicing machines. Only in Africa does the concern remain for bankers that many countries will not be able to keep up debt repayments at current levels.

From the coverage in the main financial journals, however, most readers would never guess that 1992 was the record year for interest payments from the third world – amounting to $125 billion, or twice the amount of 'aid'(see Table 14). Nor that the total debt has never ceased growing until it now totals $1.6 trillion. Nor that indebted countries are still undergoing 'structural adjustment' programmes purely to increase their ability to repay loans to the international lending institutions.

Table 14: Interest Payments on Third World Debt 1980–94

| | US$ to the nearest billion | | | | | | | |
	1980	1985	1987	1989	1990	1991	1992	1994
Interest*	48	79	85	104	112	113	125	119

*Interest = interest on long and short term debt and IMF loans plus interest arrears for the current year which is added to the total owed.
Source: World Bank Debt Tables (1991 to year 1991) (1994 for years 1992 and 1994)

Structural adjustment programmes designed by the major powers acting within the IMF and executed via the IMF and World Bank – both successful, profit-making institutions of the rich world (despite their titles) – are the globalisation of neo-liberal and anti-social ideology and policies. Despite protests, structural adjustment programmes are ongoing and are still being proposed and executed by compliant governments and the beneficiary multinational corporations.

Still it is the lowest paid and weakest, often women, who have to pay a disproportionate amount of the debt. At the level of organised labour, trade unionists and social movement leaders have paid with their lives in many countries to oppose the anti-social provisions of these programmes. Not only have these programmes undermined the livelihood of workers and the poor, they have also concentrated their attacks on publicly provided services, particularly in Africa and Latin America. One-by-one the models of 'structurally adjusted' economies are leading to poverty, social unrest or even civil war.

Chile is one such country – indeed, the first model of a structurally adjusted economy. Handed over to the 'Chicago boys' to conduct a living experiment in their 'free market' economic theories, Chile's suffering people were forced to accept the dubious status of pioneers of the new economic age under the draconian military regime of Pinochet. The results have been publicised as a complete vindication of privatisation and 'free market' ideologies. True, the virtual reality of the Chilean production economy was higher economic growth, lower debt and increased openness to the world economy. But at what cost and toward what end?

First, Chile, like other Latin American countries, had to sell its non-renewable resources at knock-down prices to appease and encourage international capital. This included everything from overfishing its waters for sardine, through environmentally careless mining to destruction of its natural stands of timber. The social onslaught raised unemployment and imposed massive cuts in public spending, while those living below the poverty line increased to 30 per cent of the population. By 1990 the poorest had seen their income drop from 20 per cent to 16 per cent while the richest 10 per cent increased their share of national income from 36 per cent to 48 per cent: a sick social economy but a healthy virtual economy as national income increased at an annual growth rate of 3 per cent or more. In 'free market' terms this is rated a success.

Throughout Latin America, and in many parts of Asia, the Chilean story has been repeated. Debt and interest are being paid out of increased growth; the rich have indeed been globalised – they would rather risk social upheaval at home than be cut off from the benefits of the global economy.

In Africa the debt burden remains and interest continues to be paid. Structural adjustment programmes play havoc with health and education and ensure that in human capital terms Africa's economic and social problems will continue for decades.

In the wake of structural adjustment policies, when women have to close the gap opened up by cuts in public services, girls stay at home to help their mothers, so that they no longer attend school.

A recent report of the UN Conference for Trade and Development (UNCTAD) concerning 'The Least Developed Countries' (LDCs), points out that for the 555 million inhabitants of the least developed countries, 'the situation (at end 1994) is worse than in the 1980s, which was regarded as a "lost decade" for the LDCs'. 'Without the benefit of sustained international support,' the report continues, 'LDCs will most probably become further marginalised as the process of globalisation gains further momentum'.

For the creditors, the debt crisis is over. For the debtors, debt bondage has been institutionalised and the pattern of world extraction determined for some time to come. This situation is changing the whole concept of North/South relations. Aid budgets and development cooperation budgets are under attack in all the donor countries. This reflects a change of morality in which all aspects of social welfare and redistribution are under attack. At the same time, however, the very point of giving aid at all is being openly questioned. 'If the poor simply get poorer despite development cooperation,' it is asked, 'why bother?'

But the wrong cause is being cited and the wrong questions are being asked. Aid must be put in the context of the other financial flows. If we do so, we can see that

- of all the financial flows, aid is the smallest;
- aid payments are only half the size of interest repayments on loans;
- aid is only one third of combined interest payments and profit repatriations from the debtor countries.

The question should therefore be asked whether, to assist the South, and especially the poorest countries, it would not be better to adjust the world economy, to make concessions in investment, technology and repayment of debt on past unproductive investments. To do so requires rethinking the international finance structures and, in particular, focussing regulatory attention on the multinationals and the transnational banks. It also implies remodelling world governance by rethinking the role of nation states, and introducing democracy and solidarity into world decision-making.

Employment: flexibility or disintegration?

There is uniform agreement that a major problem of the world social economy is unemployment. G7 (the grouping of the seven major industrialised nations in the world) has already held a meeting on employment and others are planned. In many ways the attention given to employment questions is an indication that the collective organisation of workers still has a resonance in political circles.

But unemployment is only one, albeit an important, indicator of economic failure. Behind this barrage of expressed concern over unemployment lies a fundamental change in the structure of employment itself. It is becoming more precarious, with free trade zones and home-based work taking over more and more. The unemployed, meanwhile, are conventionally defined as people seeking work, and sometimes only as those job-seekers who have previously been in paid, structured and secure employment. This definition therefore excludes all those people who are in the so-called informal sector – casual, own-account, family labour, independent occupations. These people are never recognised as unemployed in the conventional sense. Indeed such workers, the majority of them women, were never recognised as employed in the first place. Their contribution is invisible.

Significantly, labour market 'flexibilisation' policies, working alongside the contract labour strategies of the major companies, have increased the percentage of such categories within the total world labour force. If these informal sector labourers are included, then the unemployment picture becomes significantly different. Thus even an industrialised country such as Italy, which has a large informal economy, would see its unemployment rate move from 10.9 to 14.6 per cent, while in developing countries the increase is many times greater.

Conventionally defined unemployment in the industrialised economies has continued at high levels even though the world production economy has shown growth in recent years. The European Union unemployment rate has remained between 8 per cent and 10 per cent since 1981 – high historical levels. At the same time, the rate of unemployment among young people in some countries is between 20 and 40 per cent of the age group. Increasing numbers of young people have never had experience of structured employment.

In industrialised countries this situation has been an open strategy of labour market 'flexibility' in which people with secure and organised jobs have been progressively replaced by casual workers through sub-contracting or 'outsourcing'. In developing countries its counterpart has been the policy of promoting the so-called 'informal sector' from its large population pool of casual workers.

Robert Reich, US Secretary of Labor and a writer on the future of work, addressed the following words on this subject to the International Labour Conference – the annual plenary of the UN's International Labour Organisation in 1994:

> I do not know what the word 'flexibility' is. Rarely in inter-national discourse has a word gone so directly from obscurity to meaninglessness without any intervening period of coherence. Some people when they talk about labour market flexibility are talking about the freedom of employers to fire workers, the freedom of employers to reduce wages. I tell you something. That kind of freedom is not going to lead to higher standards of living in any of our countries.

Yet informalisation and unemployment persist and accelerate – by no means least in the USA (see Table 15).

A hierarchy of workers is being created – a pyramid – at the top of which are regular paid workers, followed in descending order by intermittent and part-time workers, independent individual sub-contractors and casual labourers in precarious and undefined work. At the very bottom of the heap are the long-term unemployed who sometimes have the chance to live on social security benefits which are also in danger of being abolished. In the last decade of the twentieth century the rela-tionship between work and income is being undermined. Top salaried workers work less and less for more and more, while those toiling at the very bottom cannot find work and must survive as best they can.

Table 15: Unemployment Rates: Industrialised Countries 1961–94

Country group	1961–70	1971–80	1981–90	1991	1992	1993	1994
Group of Seven	3.1	4.6	5.9	6.2	6.7	6.9	7.0
United States	5.6	6.5	6.4	6.6	7.3	6.7	6.5
Japan	1.1	1.6	2.1	2.1	2.1	2.5	2.9
European Union	2.1	4.6	8.0	8.3	9.0	10.2	10.7
Western Europe	2.0	4.3	7.4	7.9	8.7	10.0	10.5

Source: UN

The pressure to move from collective employment contracts to individual contracts as part of so-called human resource management is a move towards greater insecurity and higher unemployment in the conventional sense of the word.

Despite these developments on the labour market which, it is claimed, allow for greater 'competition' between workers, certain aspects of workers' conditions have remained very stable and structured. Even in the European Union, for example, average female net earnings are still only 50 per cent of male earnings. Migrants and racial and ethnic groups are still in a segmented labour market and disproportionately occupy the lowest paid jobs.

In developing countries job-creation should at least keep up with population growth but instead it has stagnated or fallen behind. But policy has made its contribution: the UN World Economic Report states unequivocally: 'A key feature of rising unemployment in the 1980s derived from the measures adopted in the context of stabilisation and adjustment programmes. Virtually all were associated with a compression of output, employment and wages in the short term.' 'Short term' indeed? As the previously respected economist John Maynard Keynes observed in a rather similar context – 'In the long run we are all dead.'

Policies directed at decreasing unemployment must accept the changed nature of work and the need for a vastly different and improved role for workers within the enterprise. Workers surely have a right to be considered as much part of the 'fixed costs' of the undertaking as machinery – rather than as a cost item to be minimised on the balance sheet. Policy makers must also accept that protection and security are as much part of human values as consumption of material goods.

If the 'virtual reality' of globalisation is not matched by a firm understanding and respect for the aspirations of workers and citizens at the level of local social reality, its survival will be short and its demise catastrophic.

Notes

1 *World Investment Report: Transnational Corporations, Employment and the Workplace*, New York, United Nations Conference on Trade and Development (UNCTAD) 1994.
2 TNCs: transnational corporations – an alternative (less used but more accurate) name for the multinational companies.
3 *Employment in Europe*, Brussels, European Commission, Directorate General for Employment, Industrial Relations and Social Affairs, 1994
4 Chase newsletter of 13 January 1995.
5 OECD Observer No. 190, October/November 1994 p. 13.

2. Unite and Organise – the way ahead for world labour

There's just going to have to be a stand-off somewhere down the line. If everyone cuts wages, nobody'll be able to buy a car. Then how are they going to sell tyres?

> Bobby Clarke, locked-out tyre production worker,
> on the picket line outside Pirelli,
> Nashville, Tennessee, March 1995.

They wouldn't be allowed to treat people in Italy like this.

> Raymond Hirsch, locked-out tyre production worker,
> on the same picket line outside Pirelli.

Everywhere, things are linking up. National economic borders are vanishing, but so are the boundaries between industrial sectors. As the big multinationals corporatise the world economy, workers have relearned globally an old, hard lesson. An injury to one is an injury to all.

The obvious conclusion is that workers must forge new links of their own – across national frontiers but also across the old sectoral divides. The merger, on 1 January 1996, between the International Federation of Chemical, Energy and General Workers' Unions and the Miners' International Federation to form the ICEM places us at a historic highpoint of opportunity. It provides a much-needed rallying point for working people and their communities as they face new challenges and new dangers. Those dangers can often seem remote. In fact, though, they are real, immediate and very close to home.

An advertisement targeted at American company executives in 1993 showed a very worried businessman. 'I can't,' he sighed, 'find good, loyal workers for a dollar an hour within a thousand miles of here'. The ad's soothing reply was: 'Yes You Can. Yucatan'. Yucatan is the Mexican state that juts up towards the United States across the Gulf of Mexico. In the advertisement, the Yucatan state government boasted that its workers cost on average 'under $1 an hour, including benefits'. This, it proudly noted, was 'far lower than in the Far East. And less than CBI [Caribbean], Central America and even less than the rest of Mexico'. US executives were urged to 'see how well you or your plant managers can live here while making your company more competitive'.

Or while shopping around for even better bargains. Investors are now moving into Burma, where workers can be hired for six dollars a *month* (when they are paid at all). Evidence is mounting that the Burmese military regime uses 'forced labour' (in other words, slaves) on the infrastructure for joint ventures with leading multinationals.

Geographically, then, we are all now in a single, but very unequal, labour market. The dangers of that in terms of pay, occupational and environmental health, fair employment conditions and, indeed, simple human decency are obvious. In addition, the new global corporate economy respects sectoral boundaries as little as it respects national frontiers.

Industrial revolutions worldwide produced – or, in some places, are now producing – a rapid specialisation of work tasks. Naturally, this sudden transformation of their waking hours also changes the way people see themselves and those around them. Human thought has always tended to move categories from one level to another, so it is understandable that industry itself came to be seen as a row of specialised, watertight boxes.

In fact, though, the work tasks never functioned in isolation, and neither did the industries. Today, the various industrial sectors are really no longer distinct at all. Part of the reason for this can be found in technological change, in the advent of new processes and new materials. But the blurring of the sectors is due above all to changes in the ownership of industry. Big corporations have rapidly expanded their industrial coverage. They have diversified horizontally and vertically by buying into new processes and product ranges whenever this suits their ends. And their ends are profits.

More recently, the privatisation process has also blurred the distinction between public and private sectors – for example, in the electricity, gas and water industries.

Exxon is an example of how ICEF and MIF membership interests overlap. Ranked the world's no. 2 multinational in terms of foreign assets held in 1992, Exxon then employed 95,000 people, of whom 59,000 were outside the USA, its 'home' country. But by no means all Exxon's workers are in its original industry, oil. It also owns mines. MIF-affiliated miners in Colombia have, over recent years, waged some hard-fought and ultimately successful industrial campaigns at an Exxon-owned mining company there. In doing so, they called upon the solidarity of unions in other Exxon subsidiaries – including oil unions affiliated to the ICEF.

The ICEF/MIF merger means that the Exxon miners are in the same International as other Exxon workers. They now have direct access to networking, research and solidarity campaigns concerning this major energy multinational. This is a good example of the trade union synergies that the world's workers must develop further in their own defence.

For, just as the big corporations seek gains through cross-sectoral links, so also they have, whenever it is to their advantage, tried to run down whole industries. And yet the destruction of our industries, our working conditions and our trade unions, is not inevitable. It can be reversed by a strong, united inter-national trade union movement. But that movement must be innovative and proactive in its own defence.

The two groups of workers united in the new International are key to the development process. They have proud histories of struggle in defence of their members' interests. Within the industrialised nation states of the nineteenth and early-twentieth centuries, industrial trade union struggles also triggered broader improvements in economic, social and political democracy. Similar developments can be seen in many newly industrialis-ing countries today. And in those of the older-established industrial democracies that have lurched to the right in recent decades, there is a growing sentiment among labour cam-paigners that new industrial union organising will have to be the forerunner of new social and political progress, rather than the other way round. The situation currently experienced by our members in large parts of the globe means that the battle for power over the process of economic and social development is as urgent now as at any time in the past.

In the national economies of the nineteenth and early-twentieth centuries, a series of checks and balances was developed. National laws, regulations, social institutions and, above all, trade unions provided some counterweight, however unequal, to the might of the companies. But in today's global economy, no such checks and balances exist. There is no world factory inspectorate. No world social legislation to check the worst excesses of the multinationals. No world government to counterbalance the world strategies of world corporations. And while workers are organised at world level (as, indeed, are consumers and environmentalists), they have not so far matched the effective globalisation achieved by capital.

The enormous change in the balance of power between global economic and national political institutions calls for a matching change in the organisation of civil society. As described in 'World Social Economy 1995', the process of world economic integration is taking place whether we like it or not. In many ways, it is already complete. That is not the issue. The problem for the trade union movement is how to upgrade its response to match the power structures of the late-twentieth century. Obviously, this cannot be done with exactly the same defence mechanisms as were forged in the industrialised countries of the nineteenth century. It does, however, mean learning from – perhaps reviving – the best of past trade union practice. In particular, it means a revival of the spirit and the commitment of our trade union forebears.

Global organisation is not the same thing as international organisation. Global organisation takes the total picture of world interactions into account and is not led by power relations between individual nations. This also illustrates the difference between the global organisation of transnational corporations and 'international relations' as practised by inter-governmental bodies such as the UN and its specialised agencies, or the new World Trade Organisation. 'International relations' are also what have been exercised up to now by the still evolving world trade union movement.

Trade unions were founded to bring about change in the unjust societies of the past. They must return to that founding role as the champions of change – but this time also on the world stage. Trade unions need to lead necessary change from the front. Negativism and defeatism in the face of difficult industrial evolution would rapidly condemn the union movement to irrelevance.

New elements of trade union action must include:

- an awareness that, above and beyond their historical relationship to national power institutions, workers everywhere depend on each other;

- a shared vision of world justice and progress.

Strength in numbers: trade union mergers

If changes in industry make trade union mergers logical and necessary at world level, naturally the same is true within each nation. Indeed, merged trade union structures at national level in many countries are helping to determine the future shape of the international movement. Examples of the reconstruction of trade union organisations at national level are multiplying at present. A wave of change is transforming old jurisdictional divisions.

The planned reformation of the Australian trade union movement has resulted in the emergence of strong new industrial groupings, sharing enhanced servicing power and delivering greater industrial 'clout' on behalf of their members. The agreed merger in Germany between the chemical and process workers' union (IG Chemie-Papier-Keramik) and the mining and energy union (IG Bergbau und Energie) is a direct parallel to the merger at international level. In Canada (chemical, energy, paper and communications), France (chemical and energy workers of the CFDT), Italy (chemical and energy workers), Netherlands (planning a broad industrial workers' federation), Spain (also a new 'allied industrial workers' federation'), Sweden (process and textile unions forming a new industrial workers' union), the process of consolidation is gathering force. Merger in 1995 between the United Rubber Workers' Union and the United Steelworkers' Union of America is the precursor of an even bigger grouping planned to include the steelworkers', autoworkers' and machinists' unions in a two-million strong combination by the year 2000.

These mergers are in part a response to the industrial changes that we have outlined. They also, of course, reflect a need to maximise trade unions' effectiveness at a time when their resources and their membership figures are under strong pressure in many parts of the world.

Organising – *the* priority

If trade unions are to restructure and regroup in a meaningful way, they need a clear sense of priorities. In most countries the priority of priorities remains what it was at the outset of the movement – basic trade union organising. Unions have to recruit again in the sectors and areas where they have lost ground. They must extend their recruitment into largely unorganised sectors and sections of the workforce.

There is no denying that unions in some countries, including some of the older-established industrial states, have in the past allowed their attention to be diverted from this essential task. They have tended to concentrate on national political structures as the main focus of trade union action. This has allowed companies time to develop a comprehensive and sophisticated response to unionisation at the enterprise level. Meanwhile, national political action has lost much of its power to deliver. Despite all the talk about 'free markets', the world now has a planned economy as never before. However it is planned not by governments or parliaments but behind the boardroom doors of the major multinational companies. To re-assert their ability to control change in the interest of workers and the communities in which they live, modern trade unions will have to develop the necesssary power relationship to the real decision networks of the global economy – the transnational corporations.

Of course, national political and legislative campaigning can still be made relevant to the defence of workers' rights. However, to be effective, trade union lobbying has to be carried out by organisations that can demonstrate their representative character. And to be representative, unions have to organise. If they do not, they will find it increasingly difficult to disprove the old lie that they are a 'special interest group'.

Organising is not the purpose of trade unionism. It is the means towards the end of defending working people and their families. But the means always predates the end. The process does not work in reverse order.

These days, effective union organising means getting organised internationally as well as locally.

Internationalising

The international industrial federations (the sector-by-sector International Trade Secretariats, or ITS) exist to build this union response at the industrial level internationally. This may seem to be a statement of the obvious, but it is sometimes forgotten that the international industrial federations are primarily organisations of industrial action, indeed of industrial struggle, rather than political lobbyists.

The industrial ITS have to become more practically front-line industrial organisations, involved from the start in national unions' industrial campaigns. All too often, the 'internationals' are brought in as fire-fighters, as a last resort when local action has failed. In the world of the multinational corporations, this is *not* the way to win industrial campaigns. Action has to be planned on an international basis right from the start. This entails a change in thinking – both within national unions and within the ITS themselves.

National trade unions and their members must recognise the transnational reality behind most current industrial operations

Certainly, this entails more information and education, but more importantly, it requires the development of an organising and campaigning orientation within the ITS. This will be facilitated by democratisation of international trade union structures. The 'centralising' view of trade union power is out of touch with reality. Ultimately, the power of any trade union structure resides in its local branches. The democratic principle means that decisions need to be locally 'owned'.

The development of labour action as a series of networks is a natural outgrowth of this recognition. Such networking is, in fact, much easier for the unions than it is for the hierarchical management side of industry. Perhaps from a recognition of this latent union strength, corporations themselves are now talking of worker involvement in the production process and of 'empowerment'. It is the job of the international trade union movement to ensure that this is true 'empowerment' rather than just the stealing of union clothes by corporate personnel departments.

The newly merged International will need to extend the 'multinational company networks' throughout the dominant multinational companies in its sectors. These networks involve the establishment of permanent communication between the International's headquarters and plant-level trade union correspondents worldwide within the company concerned. The aim is to build overall knowledge of the company's production, strategies, industrial relations policies and collective bargaining performance – and to ensure that all on the network are in possession of this overview. This should be a convincing demonstration that an industrial trade union international is not a remote bureaucracy, but an essential provider of data and information for concrete, day-to-day trade union work. These days, such networks often use computers. They are not, however, essentially 'computer networks'. The computers are one possible medium, not the message.

This strategy will, of course, entail a greater commitment of resources, as well as longer-term strategic planning of such structures: they must not become mere company-dominated 'information exchanges'. This is a real danger, as is illustrated by the reported remarks of Martin Apsel in 1995. The *Financial Times* of 27 July 1995 noted that Apsel, formerly European director of industrial relations for General Motors, the world's largest multinational, had been responsible for developing GM's policy on works councils. According to the *Financial Times*, he told a private meeting of personnel managers, held in Ireland during July 1995, that GM's decision to set up a works council for all its European plants was intended as a safeguard against the spread of high German labour costs. He reportedly added that the aim of GM's policy on this issue was 'to contain the influence of the German unions'. The *Financial Times* said that Apsel's speech was secretly taped and an unauthorised transcript passed to a British trade union. Unless the European Works Councils, or any transnational councils that may be constructed, serve a *trade union* purpose and are part of a conscious *trade union* strategy from the outset, they will be more of a hindrance than a help to the workers they aim to represent.

The longer-term trade union aim of the International's multinational company networks should be entirely independent of any regional, national or other institutional agenda. Simply put, the aim should be to engage the multinationals in negotiated exchanges with trade unions at the global level. These companies are, after all, the nexus of modern economic and, to an increasingly uncomfortable extent, political power. The networks can develop the detailed information and membership awareness to bring negotiated exchanges about. This does not imply international collective bargaining over wages, but it does mean finding a way to enforce minimum codes of behaviour and agreed international standards at the company level worldwide. Such matters as common standards of protection for health and safety in common processes are inherently international. So are environmental standards. So are standards against the use of forced labour and child labour. So is the right to form and to join trade unions – which, in fact, is a basic human right, listed as such

in the Universal Declaration of Human Rights. 'Chameleon corporations' must become a thing of the past. Such companies
behave as responsible employers where local regulations and
trade union power oblige them to – but they are red in tooth
and claw wherever such constraints are inadequate.

As it is the companies that will actually change the industrial
and social scene – not the relatively less powerful governments
– it is first and foremost with the companies that trade unions
have to establish a negotiating relationship.

An example of what can be achieved in this field is the
pioneering agreement signed in 1994 between the food, agri-
culture and allied workers' international, the IUF, and the
French-based food multinational Danone. This commits both
parties to monitor the observance of trade union rights specified
by the UN's International Labour Organisation (ILO) in all
Danone subsidiaries worldwide. The agreement states that
management and unions should also negotiate and publicise
collective bargaining agreements and ensure that union repre-
sentatives enjoy equal access to skills training and promotion.
Previous worldwide framework agreements between the IUF
and Danone concern skills training, access to information and
promoting gender equality. The company and the IUF meet each
year to assess progress on the implementation of the agreements.

The International Trade Secretariats must cooperate and reform within a new framework

The creation of the ICEM is a celebration of unity, but also a
reflection of the hard industrial facts. Worldwide, as well as
nationally and locally, the employer side no longer recognises
sectoral divisions between trades, production areas or areas of
ownership.

In its developed locations, the mining industry is now just
as dependent on high technology as are the power generation,
chemicals and process industries. At the same time, the families
making matches and fireworks in the developing economies face
exploitation every bit as crude and dangerous as that suffered

by the men, women and children who mine and quarry in the same regions.

The ICEF/MIF merger is one step towards greater international trade union unity. In this respect, it should be viewed together with such recent initiatives as the plantation and agricultural workers' merger with the IUF and the closer grouping of Internationals in the media and allied groups.

Clearly, though, this cannot be the end of the process. A logical structure would be to group industrial union Internationals within some form of cooperative relationship. Whatever form this closer cooperation might take, it should be designed to bring about a sharing of resources so that wasteful duplication of effort and expertise can be avoided. There are many fields in which efforts can usefully be pooled, ranging from collective bargaining data, through joint training initiatives, to fully coordinated solidarity action on occupational health and safety. However, such cooperation will obviously not be determined by cold logic alone, but also by political and other less tangible factors.

A firmer definition is now needed of the respective roles of the ITS and the International Confederation of Free Trade Unions (ICFTU)

The fading of the old Cold War trade union rivalries – and notably the rapid withering of the former communist-led World Federation of Trade Unions – leaves the ICFTU well-placed to take on its role of providing a progressive, identifiable trade union voice within the inter-governmental agencies. If geared and motivated to do so, the ICFTU will certainly be able to bring considerable resources to bear on this important task. It would, however, have to do so in a combative way. It cannot simply be a foil for neo-liberal apologists, nor can it act as a 'loyal opposition' within institutions that are fundamentally unjust. The actions and policies of the IMF and the World Bank, for example, need challenging, not analysing.

The ITS' action, meanwhile, should be focussed mainly on the industry and enterprise level. They should concern themselves with building practical links between workers; with actual pay and conditions; with supporting actual industrial disputes; with the application of occupational safety and health protections in individual industries and global companies; and so on.

Regionalisation

Today, most International Trade Secretariats are well beyond the 'think tank' stage. The facts of the global economy are now undisputed and the need to construct an effective international labour response is accepted, at least in theory, by trade unions everywhere.

This must, however, be a flexible, interdependent response based on mutual respect between trade union movements everywhere. Never again should we witness a world labour monolith striving to concentrate all power within its own crumbling centre. The strategy of the ICEM must be 'owned' locally, by every affiliated trade union. But at the same time, every affiliate must be secure in the knowledge that it has behind it the backing and the resources of the whole International.

This has implications for the process of making and sharing decisions within the International, and thus for its structures. The fact that neither of the precursor organisations had regional structures in place is, in many ways, an advantage. The new International can design a structure that suits the present-day needs of the organisation.

The ICEM's **Executive Committee** will be structured on a regional basis. In future, its members will be elected from the regions on the sole basis of representational strength within the International. The new statutes will empower groups of members within the International to form regional structures. The task of the International and its Executive Committee will be to explore and plan ways in which various inputs can be combined into a flexible but always united whole. It is hoped that the major regions will form their own coordinating structures both for general regional representation and for specific sectoral work.

In time, these regional structures will demand **servicing**. This is a resource problem that the new International will need to address. Some of its regions may reasonably be expected to carry most of their cost burdens themselves, but others will undoubtedly need direct assistance. The new International will, fortunately, inherit local coordinators in most, though not all, regions. These coordinators can form the basis for further servicing as the necessary structures and activities are developed.

The challenge of regionalisation is to **decentralise some activity while maintaining worldwide cohesion and identity**. This is the cooperative regionalism of labour and has nothing in common with the spurious 'competitive regionalisation' promoted by the world's economic and political blocs. Neither must it be seen as a way of insulating the International as a whole from difficult discussions about, for example, migrant workers or the desirability of 'social clauses' in international trade agreements, which impact differently on different groups of workers. Rather, it must be a common mechanism for tackling common concerns – not least when workers in different regions are being lured by employers into imagining that their interests conflict.

The international trade union movement must be convinced that the cause of labour is indivisible. Without that assurance, it will be no match for the multinationals.

Striking the right balance between regional action and global strategy requires good **communications**. Both the ICEF and the MIF have been among the pioneers of electronic mail as an international trade union mobiliser. Now, the expanded possibilities offered by the Internet and the World Wide Web must be used to the full in labour's cause.

Union-building has been a priority for the MIF and the ICEF and will continue to be so for the new International. In other words, it will provide help for self-help by workers who are setting out to organise unions. Its **training** activities will therefore also have to be consciously directed towards this aim: courses must be enabling, not didactic. Above all, they must recognise that, however well they may have worked in one country, trade union and industrial relations systems can rarely be transferred lock, stock and barrel to another. Neither trade union imperialism nor touristic globetrotting have any place in today's labour movement.

Representation

While organising and union-building must be priorities for the ICEM, representation of workers' interests at the world level obviously remains a vital function. Here, the task is to build a **progressive trade union voice** on matters of industrial and general social concern. If unions keep quiet on the wider issues (for example, the environment), they will receive scant thanks from employers and governments for their restraint, but will be condemned by the community for their impotence.

Trade unions are still among the few democratically organised bodies in society. They must make strategic use of their strength. It should be the trade unions that promote sustainable, democratically decentralised patterns of industrial development – in stark contrast to the exploitative, over-centralised approach of the big corporations.

A wider public must receive the message that trade unions are society's main guarantors of social and economic democracy. The ICEM will have to confirm that image by its work with the general **media** and by further increasing its own **publishing** efforts. Considerable experience has already been gained of using electronic mail and computer bulletin boards for news releases. The new possibilities offered by the Internet and the World Wide Web will be increasingly important both for media relations and for the International's own publishing. If worldwide electronic networking continues to develop freely, there is real scope for a democratisation of the media. The direct international communication of news and ideas is a technical opportunity that the International must quickly seize. It must ensure that it has the technical and staff resources to expand its output of news items both to the media and to the general public.

There is evidence that ICEF/MIF media work to date has begun to bear fruit, notably in relation to the specialised press in the new International's sectors. Reasonably enough, media interest is greatest when real expertise is shown on a given subject. Only by generating its own, original, information, only by proving that it has a tale to tell, can a union international even hope to impress the media. This is a further reason for expanding the ICEM's research capacities, as discussed below. If the International can provide the facts, the message will be the more impressive.

Meanwhile, the International must also build up its own publishing programme of magazines and specialised reports. And it must get them to the public at large. Otherwise, it runs the risk of preaching to the converted only. Attracting a wider readership entails further improvement of presentation – not in lavish self-advertisement, but as an effective means of putting across an often rather unfamiliar message. Joint ventures with commercial publishers, a technique of which the ICEF has already gained some experience, are another promising way forward.

The International must also be ready to **debate and, where appropriate, form alliances with other social groups** (political parties that share its outlook, environmental organisations, women's organisations, youth organisations, human rights networks, organisations of the self-employed and of the unemployed and, perhaps on some issues, consumer organisations). But to do so, the ICEM must first define its own ground and enter into debate with its own objectives clearly agreed. This implies **input from trade union workshops and discussion groups** at the local, regional and international industrial levels.

The International must work with the **inter-governmental structures** to raise and defend their ability to control the multi-nationalisation process. This applies in particular to the UN, and more especially to those of its agencies and programmes that are of direct relevance to the International – for example, the International Labour Organisation (ILO), the World Health Organisation (WHO) and the United Nations Environment Programme (UNEP). The aim must be to strengthen these agencies' ability to set and to enforce standards. In a global economy, international standards have to become more than codes of conduct. They must be given real teeth. To achieve this will take solid trade union groundwork and follow-up. Here too, the International needs to advance a proactive trade union strategy in world affairs.

Effectiveness

The ICEM will be the forerunner of the new global institutions of labour. It must be an enabling mechanism:

- a rallying point for solidarity when needed;
- a forum for exchanging diverse views, comparing interests and finding solutions;
- a collection point for information, analysis and forward-looking solutions;
- a service centre of human resources for exchange and interaction;
- a pool for practical assistance (fund-raising for project work, training expertise, mutual advice).

Some of the main means to these ends are:

- Efficient research, storage and retrieval of specific trade union and collective bargaining information. Means have now been well developed to retrieve information for affiliated trade unions concerning the structures, ownership and performance of companies. However, no commercial databases exist that can provide the information that affiliates most often need on wages, working conditions and specific contract language. This work must be undertaken by the International itself. The multinational company networks discussed above will be the starting point for the collection and analysis of such data.

    This information is, however, only one aspect of collective bargaining support. Past experience with on-the-spot assistance by experts used to the particular company's management or the particular techniques under discussion has been among the best examples of exchange between affiliates. One important task for the International is to identify and catalogue sources of expertise that can be drawn on when needed.

- Activities led by policy and purpose. 'Grant-chasing' must be no part of the International's brief. Naturally, at a time of scarce resources, additional funding is always to be welcomed. But the money must be for activities that the International can and should undertake in support of its core objectives. Funds must be sought for programmes. Programmes should not be manufactured to attract funds. This may sometimes mean that the International will have to convince donor agencies themselves to change their criteria if they do not correspond to the real needs of our members.

- Occupational and environmental health and safety – from information to action. On health and safety, too, some of the most valued assistance has come from those with direct expertise in reviewing plant operations and helping to negotiate corrective solutions with local management. A resource base of experts on occupational health and safety and environmental audits is being built and extended. This area of work is also providing potential breakthroughs in relations with multinational companies. Direct discussion fora have been established between representative unions, the International and multinational corporate man-agements in certain sectors to negotiate universal minimum health and safety standards, trade union involvement in monitoring and enforcement, and provisions for health and safety training. If successful, these initiatives could provide a jumping-off point for further negotiating potential at the global level, based on mutual recognition and understanding.

- Sector conferences will continue to bind affiliated trade unions in specific industries together. They also assist information exchange and provide invaluable personal contacts between trade unionists from different countries in the same sector. In addition, however, the International will need to create more opportunities for joint strategy discussions in response to the effects on collective bargaining and work organisation of the industrial developments already described.

- Membership development must continue – both into unorganised sections of the workforce and into new geographical constituencies. The ICEF and MIF have successfully taken on the challenge of the new developments in Central and Eastern Europe. The rapid industrialisation of China and India faces the ICEM with even greater tasks. Resources have not kept pace with this vast growth in organising scope. Although the MIF's and ICEF's work grew enormously after the opening up of Central and Eastern Europe, the internationals' revenues shrank as a result of pressures on membership elsewhere. If the new International is to successfully confront the challenges of a new world, fresh resources will have to be found. Ways of achieving this may include better dues payment discipline by affiliates of the ICEM, a rise in fees per capita (although this has often simply resulted in reduced collection rates), or more imaginative ways of providing revenue from services at the international level.

- The International must develop new approaches to trade union intervention at the enterprise level. Discussion of new approaches to the control and ownership of enterprises should be accelerated. This is all the more necessary in view of the wholly different past and present experience of workers in Eastern Europe and China. These regions are not likely to reproduce the recent economic and social history of other parts of the world. With the right impetus, a new socially directed post-capitalism could emerge worldwide, in which the idea will be prominent that each enterprise should be 'owned' by those who work in it and by the society on behalf of which it functions. Modern management is already modifying its structures in order, for example, to give Board representation to community groups – even, in a few cases, to environmentalists. Yet at the same time, those selfsame corporate managements are seeking to weaken organised labour in the mine and the plant by means of subcontracting and the introduction of new work organisation techniques.

Current developments at world level reflect an attempt by the owners of capital and their professional managers to force social activity to conform to their own short-sighted aims. In the long term, this is no basis for maintaining a consensus on development. The trade union movement should be coming forward with the alternative view of an enterprise community where people who have invested their work in a firm have at least the same rights as people who have invested their money, a community of stakeholders rather than stockholders. Certainly, the unions must spend time and effort on finding positive labour alternatives for economic and social development.

Technological and economic development is *not* mechanistic and related to mystic factors buried deep in academic jargon. Economic and technical change responds directly to social power. If, as at present, this development is skewed to serve exclusively private interests instead of broader social ends, it is because excessive power rests in corporate hands. This imbalance must be corrected. Trade unions need to build a response rooted in the defence of workers and their community – and integrated from the local branch right through to the International. For world labour, the way ahead is clear:
UNITE AND ORGANISE.

3. Founding Declaration of the International Federation of Chemical, Energy, Mine and General Workers Unions (ICEM), Washington DC, 22 November 1995

The foundation of the International Federation of Chemical, Energy, Mine and General Workers' Unions, the ICEM, is a new departure for world trade unionism. Member organisations of the former MIF and ICEF will blend the best of their traditions and aspirations into a new international trade union federation. This new international will be a powerful body capable of acting decisively on behalf of the workers it represents into the twenty-first century and beyond. A global organisation, it will focus on achieving practical results and gains for its members. Strength is its sinew, service its duty, action its day-to-day business. Solidarity in practice, permanently renewed and strengthened, is the ICEM's driving force.

The ICEM represents workers who extract, transform and produce vast quantities of the world's requirements and riches. Its membership works at the forefront of industrial activity in a wide range of industries including: chemicals, energy, mining and quarrying, pulp and paper, rubber, glass, ceramics, cement, environmental services and other services. It represents manufacturing and production workers, administrative, clerical, scientific, professional, supervisory and technical staff in these industries. The industrial logic and breadth of its coverage represent a major source of the ICEM's strength and legitimacy.

The grip of transnational corporate power on the world economy is a phenomenon which did not exist when the ICEF and the MIF were created. Under the new and powerful influence of the transnational corporations, governments have often become mere agencies to facilitate the free flow of capital, technology, information and products. The real needs and wants of working men and women are ignored in the balance sheets of corporate giants. Unemployment and destitution are still on the increase. Child labour and forced labour continue to shame human decency. Wars and conflicts are still raging. The arms race is not yet over.

National, regional and local trade union issues must now be addressed from an international perspective. Within the sectors it represents, the ICEM will face these issues squarely, with effective policies and programmes.

Exploitation of workers continues. In many parts of the world, this abuse is at least as crude as anything seen in the last century. Combating exploitation, discrimination and poverty today and in the future requires powerful and refined means, as well as a renewed sense of urgency and commitment. The ICEM will develop both the means and the commitment needed to champion change in defence of its members. Similarly, it will spearhead the promotion and defence of trade union rights in its sectors as an integral part of the broader fight for basic human rights.

The ICEM will have the resources to develop a new power relationship with the real decision networks of an ever more integrated world, whether those networks be corporate or governmental. The ICEM will actively represent its members in all fora where their interests are at stake. It will forge the necessary alliances with other groups of international civil society sharing the same basic aims.

The ICEM is committed to safeguarding the health and safety of its members and the sustainability of the world environment. In this respect its commitment goes beyond the immediate interests of its members and encompasses the interests of their families and the broader community.

In all its activities and in its decision-making, the ICEM will actively promote equal rights and opportunities for women, not least by making women's contribution more visible.

The ICEM hereby dedicates itself to the following six principles:

Commitment

The trade union movement has a soul. The ICEM is driven in its activities by the will to right wrongs and injustice. It has at heart the real lives and problems of people.

The ICEM is committed to achieve positive and progressive change in the lives of working men and women, in their communities and in society at large. It is morally engaged on the side of the exploited, the poor, the downtrodden and the victims of discrimination. This commitment will express itself in prompt responses to the requests of all member-organisations and in untiring efforts to reach the goals set by its Congress of members.

Solidarity

International trade union solidarity is about finding shared solutions to problems that arise. It is the single most important weapon for winning improvements globally. It is a permanent and proactive process of sharing resources, companionship and objectives. Solidarity is not just proclaimed. It must be built, permanently consolidated and demonstrated in practice.

Through its global relations with the rest of the international democratic trade union movement, the ICEM will be an essential link in the vast chain of international workers' solidarity. The ICEM will be a unique means for member organisations to give and receive international solidarity. It will seek constantly to improve the quality and effectiveness of its own solidarity action. It will favour the forging of direct ties with like-minded individuals and organisations.

Justice is not to be found everywhere and forever. It is won by continuously fighting oppression in all its forms. Both within the organisation and in its relations with the rest of the world, the ICEM will fight for justice and equality and will itself be even-handed and just.

The ICEM will be its member unions' watchdog to ensure acceptance and application of relevant international law and standards.

Democracy

The legitimacy of the international trade union movement derives from its elected structures and the democratic nature of its decision-making. Policies of the ICEM are decided and owned by representative national and local trade unions and their members. This specific feature distinguishes the international trade union movement from many other voluntary organisations and confers on it authority, credibility and responsibility.

The ICEM will constantly strive to strengthen the checks and balances that are essential to internal democracy. The organis-ation secures its income from fees paid by its members. It will ensure the proper management of its income and the imple-mentation of the decisions of its governing bodies in an accountable and transparent way.

As part of its efforts to strengthen internal democracy and bring the decision-making process as close as possible to its members, the ICEM will introduce a regionalised structure and increase regional exchanges and activities.

Information

The ICEM will base its activities on a unique mastery of the policies, facts and figures which matter for its member organ-isations. This capability will deliver good, timely data and analyses which are relevant to its members and are not readily available elsewhere. The ability to provide data on collective bargaining, wages, industry trends and corporate changes can help member organisations to improve the working and living conditions of their members. This is the ultimate objective of all the ICEM's information and research.

This aim can be achieved only if all participate in the global effort. Member unions will express their needs and will provide structured information when requested. They will also show preparedness to share, with others who need it, the expertise that has been built within their organisations. The ICEM itself will concentrate on gathering and analysing sector-specific data with a strong emphasis on labour conditions and related matters.

Organising

An organisation founded on deeply-held principles still needs to build the power to act on them. Acquiring know-how and the capacity to articulate clearly their needs and wants, building strong and sound organisations, and promoting and defending the rights and conditions of all workers are therefore vital to the empowerment of workers and their organisations.

The strength of argument and the argument of strength go hand-in-hand when combating exploitation and poor working conditions. Acquiring the capacity to propose their own solutions and the power to oppose, influence or enter into partnerships, as and when necessary, is what unions need in order to be effective at local and national level.

The ICEM will be at the forefront of this struggle internationally.

Effectiveness

The ICEM's resources will remain limited, but the needs of its affiliates are immense. In allocating resources and carrying out activities, the ICEM will constantly seek to make the best possible use of its resources in order to achieve the best possible results. Professionalism, commitment and quality will be the hallmark of the ICEM's services, and each of its campaigns and programmes will be strategically planned with a view to being result-oriented.

The ICEM's agenda and programmes will be set with the sole aim of assisting its affiliates. It will also join campaigns and participate in events which are of direct relevance to its affiliates and their members.

To achieve these aims, trade unions everywhere must unite the organised workers and organise the unorganised.

Therefore, on this historic founding day of a new industrial trade union international, the ICEM and its affiliated trade unions worldwide solemnly recommit themselves to:
UNITE AND ORGANISE.

Appendix

Membership of the International Trade Secretariats, November 1995

	Number of workers represented	Number of affiliated trade unions	Number of countries
International Federation of Building and Woodworkers (IFBWW)	11500000	227	102
International Federation of Chemical, Energy, Mine and General Workers' Unions (ICEM) [On 1 Jan. 1996]	20000000	403	113
International Federation of Commercial, Clerical and Technical Employees (FIET)	11300000	400	120
Universal Alliance of Diamond Workers (UADW)	30000	9	8
Education International (EI)	23000000	258	140
International Secretariat of Entertainment Trade Unions (ISETU)	200000	113	63
International Union of Food, Agricultural, Hotel, Restaurant, Catering, Tobacco and Allied Workers' Associations (IUF)	2600000	312	110
International Graphical Federation (IGF)	2000000	100	68
International Federation of Journalists (IFJ)	400000	117	91
International Metalworkers' Federation (IMF)	18000000	180	90
Postal, Telegraph and Telephone International (PTTI)	4298943	254	112
Public Services International (PSI)	20000000	436	126
International Textile, Garment and Leather Workers' Federation (ITGLWF)	7000000	200	100
International Transport Workers' Federation	4393338	476	120

Source: Each organisation's own figures, collected in an ICEM telephone survey.